# THIS BOOK BELONGS TO

## *The Library of*

...................................................................

...................................................................

Thank you for Purchasing my book and taking the time to read it from front to back. I am always grateful when a reader chooses my work and I hope you enjoyed it!

With the vast selection available online, I am touched that you chose to be purchasing my work and take valuable time out of your life to read it. My hope is that you feel you made the right decision.

I very much would like to know what you thought of the book. Please take the time to write an honest and informative review on Amazon.com. Your experience and opinions will be of great benefit to me and those readers looking to make an informed choice.

*With much thanks.*

# Table of Contents

# Introduction:

How many times per day do you check Facebook? How many videos do you start watching that you hadn't even planned to watch?

How many times do you click from one thing to the next without consciously realizing what you're doing. How many posts, videos and photos do you like in a day?

People are sharing everything on the different social media sites, from pictures of their children to job postings to world news and more! Everything that is going on in the world around us, whether on a small or large scale, can be found on the numerous social media platforms that we use every day, and there do not seem to be any signs of this slowing down. Every day, social media is growing; new people are creating their first social media account, and others are creating accounts on multiple platforms. The odds of social media becoming a thing of the past are slim to none. Whether we like it or not, social media is here to stay.

With all of this in mind, would it not make sense to use social media in the business world? Nearly everyone - billions of people - have at least one type of social media account up and running. What better place to show the world your brand and the things that you are capable of creating? Each social media platform available provides its own unique way of broadcasting your brand to the millions (or billions) of people in the vast virtual audience. It only makes sense to jump in and use social media for your brand's advantage.

The number of Facebook users in the United States alone has reached more than 214 million earlier this year (reference 1), and that number is only expected to keep growing. For nearly as long as Facebook has existed, people have been sharing business information. With the introduction of ads in 2013, the business side of Facebook has increased steadily, and the same goes for other social media platforms such as Twitter, Instagram, and Pinterest. As a small business, how can you tap into the social media market to benefit your brand?

In the pages that follow, you can learn to use social media platforms to launch and grow your business. You can learn how to thrive on social media and expand your customer base, all while increasing awareness for your brand and fine-tuning your marketing skills. We will start from the foundation, helping you to build a strong brand that fully encapsulates what your business is about and the values at the center of it. Then we will shift our focus from the brand to the audience before helping you to develop a social media presence and use it to enhance your outreach. You will learn how to efficiently use social media to increase your return on investment (ROI) and put money in your business' pocket.

Do you want to get the absolute most out of social media for the sake of your brand? Do you want to build a relationship with your target audience that will lead to greater success for your business? Do you want to get your product or service into the public eye and further the mission of your company? We want to help you get there. Together, we will work through the 9 Chapters that follow. The first part of the book is all about branding. It will teach you how to build your brand (whether personal or business) from the ground up, and then how to find, narrow down, and target your audience. The second part of the book is all about how to build your brand on social media and how to become a social media powerhouse. With a strong brand and a strong following, the sky is the limit for you. So, shall we get started?

# Chapter 1: Define Your Brand

We see all sorts of different brands throughout our daily lives in the foods we eat, the products we use, the cars we drive, and more. We all have specific brands that we prefer to use over others, even though the products that fall under those brands are generally pretty similar. What is it that makes us decide which brands to try initially and stick with for the long haul? What makes one brand better than another?

Think of your relationship with your favorite brands that you use regularly - what made you choose those brands to begin with? What was it that first appealed to you before you decided to choose that product or service? Once it earned your favor, what was it that made you come back for more? What makes you loyal to those favorite brands instead of their competitors?

The decisions you make while creating a brand for your business are some of the most lasting and important decisions you will make throughout the lifespan of your company. Your brand is the identity of your business - it is the face, voice, and personality of your products and services, and the impression it leaves on customers will determine your business' overall value within your market and among competing businesses. Therefore, it is crucial to develop a brand that effectively captures the essence of the business and stick with the image you have created for it. Effectively branding your business can make all the difference when it comes to the success of your products and/or services.

The branding process can be exciting, but it also requires patience as a successful brand cannot be created overnight - it takes time, effort, and teamwork. The members of your business and branding team need to share an understanding of the goal in front of you and the work needed to be put in. The process might not always be easy, but the relationship with your customers that will result from your labor will be worth it.

## Essential Elements of Brand Definition

So, how do you build a successful and meaningful brand for your business? The first thing you need to do is develop a good understanding of the different aspects of your business so that the brand effectively captures its essence. Why did you start the business? Who are you helping, and with what? What is the ultimate goal your business should aim to achieve? Being able to answer these questions is important for successful business branding.

## The "Why" Behind Your Company

It is easy to point out which particular products or services have resulted from which brands - *Apple* created the iPod, *Sony* created the PlayStation, and *McDonald's* created the Big Mac - but it is not quite as easy to identify the reason behind the brand's foundation. One thing that has been proven time and time again in the business industry is that the motivation to make money does not alone lead to long-term success. So, why? Why bother entering into competition with countless other brands and risk falling on your face? Why should customers care more about your business than one that belongs to someone else?

## The Golden Circle

The most successful businesses worldwide have an excellent grasp on why they do what they do and follow the "Golden Circle" business concept developed by Simon Sinek (https://startwithwhy.com/). As you can see in the diagram below, there are three tiers to this concept: what, how, and why.

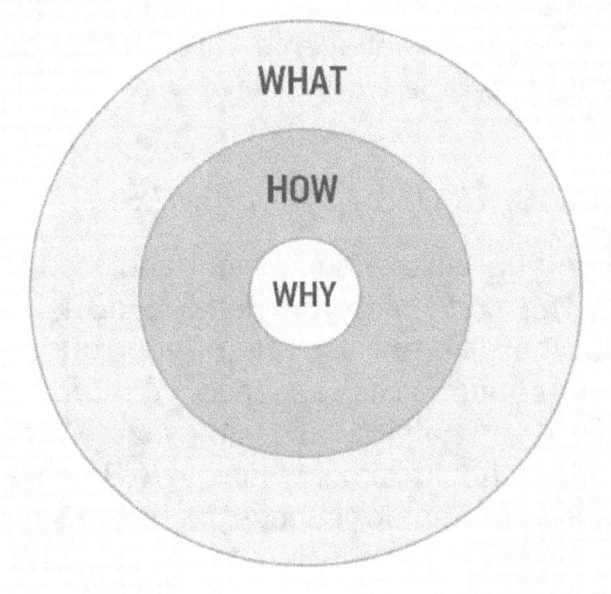

Image courtesy of **tools**hero, Golden Circle by Simon Sinek. (https://www.toolshero.com/leadership/golden-circle-simon-sinek/)

All businesses know **what** they do - how else could they follow through with what needs to be done? Essentially, every business offers a product and/or service to their target audience. However, the product or service is not the cause for the business to exist, but merely the result of the business' existence. The result of the business is the most visible component to customers, competitors, and everyone else outside the business.

Fewer businesses know **how** they do what they do - they understand the physical processes, of course, but they do not understand what it is that sets them apart from their competitors. How things are done within the business should be what differentiates it from other businesses - otherwise, everyone would be doing the exact same thing in the exact same way, and there would not be a point of having multiple businesses exist. Without understanding how the business functions differently than other similar businesses, maintaining permanent success is not possible. Many people can readily understand what a business does after a very small amount of investigation, but how the business functions isn't as obvious but can still be understood with a bit of effort.

Even fewer businesses know **why** they do what they do - the deeper purpose behind their products and services. These businesses understand that the financial reward is not the primary goal, and the fulfillment of their cause or belief takes the front seat. The "why" behind the business should be at the core of the organization - the foundation for the rest of the business functions to stand on.

The heart of the Golden Circle concept is that the "why" of the business should be more important than the "how" or the "what." Anyone can make a useful product that appeals to the general public - it is the story behind it and the motivation of the creator that sells the product. Your brand requires you to understand and value the "what" and the "how," but a successful brand is driven by the "why."

## Your Brand's Mission
The "why" behind your business is exactly what you need to decide on in order to create your brand's mission statement. The

mission statement clearly states the purpose of the business, which should be reflected in the voice, message, and personality of the brand. Think about the core values of your business - what is the passion that drives the business? What was your motivation for creating the business in the first place? Crafting a clear and understandable expression of your business' passion is one of the first steps in pushing your brand forward.

Your mission statement will be a useful tool in the future of your business; it motivates your employees and helps them to understand the point of the work they are doing, and it encourages potential customers to trust in the product and/or service you are providing them with. Everything you do within your business should align with your mission statement - you want the consistency to run through your brand so that everything works together properly.

Let's look at *Nike* as an example: the *Nike* swoop is easily recognizable, and their tagline, "Just Do It." is even known by people who do not buy their products. But what is their ultimate goal (or mission)? "To bring inspiration and innovation to every athlete in the world." They do this by creating quality products, carefully selecting famous athletes to endorse their products, and using marketing tactics that enable the viewer to see themselves with those products. The technology they use to inspire and create their products combined with the use of influential athletes from different countries combines innovation and inspiration to reach their target audience. Their mission statement matches the execution methods they use.

So, what do you need to keep in mind while creating your mission statement? Firstly, your business' passion, followed by the demographic of your target audience and the needs they are looking to have fulfilled by your product.

**Tell Your Story**

Now that you have your mission statement and a good grasp of the "why" behind your business, it is time to tell the rest of your story. Stories bring people together, build relationships, and humanize us. A good story keeps people engaged and holds their attention. Your story should inspire your target audience to commit to your brand and form a connection between you and your customers.

So, how should you put your story together? Think about the person (or people) who have already benefited the most from your business and achieved significant success because of it (every story needs a hero at the center). Emphasize the struggle that existed in the life of your hero before finding your business, and share how their mission aligned with that of your business. The story of your business contains smaller stories within it that can inspire more potential customers to take a chance on your business.

For example, back in 2000, *Subway* launched a new advertising campaign featuring a man named Jared Fogle, the story being that Mr. Fogle lost over 200 pounds by sticking to a diet consisting of *Subway* sandwiches. 200 plus pounds is no small feat for someone to overcome, and *Subway* used this story of success to their benefit by integrating it into their business' story. Mr. Fogle acted as a spokesperson for *Subway* for 15 years, and his success story helped *Subway* to gain a positive reputation for having a healthy alternative to fast food, earning them millions of dollars over the course of his advertising campaigns.

Now is the time to find your story's hero. Dig through your records from the past year and find the customers that have benefited the most from your product and/or service. Of these customers, whose success story are you the proudest of? Find your business' hero and create your story.

**Determine Your Audience**

Odds are, you had a target audience in mind when you created the idea for your business - if you had an idea for a new type of baby stroller, you probably were not thinking about marketing to senior citizens, right? The strength of your brand will depend on its identifiability with your target audience. To really focus on being a business that your customers can identify with, you will have to create a specific image in your head of the characteristics they have so that you can better understand what will appeal to them. Your target audience will likely expand to different niches as your brand grows and develops new products and/or services, but in the beginning stages, it is best to be as specific as possible about who you are trying to reach.

That being said, determine your target audience - is it, upper-class businessmen? Single parents with young children? Teenage athletes looking for a sports scholarship? What are the typical behaviors of your demographic? What can these people generally be counted on to be interested in, whether out of necessity or personal interest? Every niche has a point of appeal - find your target audience's and use it to your advantage. Knowing how to appeal to your target audience will be useful in attracting and keeping loyal customers. Customize your brand so that it appeals to the specific demographic that you are hoping to attract.

## Define What Your Brand Offers

When you are just starting out in your business, you likely do not have a lot of disposable funds. Trying to keep costs low can be frustrating, so try to focus on what you do have. In order to start your business, you had to have a great idea and turn it into something bigger - that is something to be proud of! While you are still in the early stages and are less distracted by the money you will be making, take the time to really pinpoint exactly what your brand offers consumers and make it into a launching pad for your business.

What makes your brand unique? What are you offering that no one else can offer? What sets your product or service apart from the competition in your field? You know who your target audience is, now show them why they should choose your brand instead of a different one.

## The Solution for Your Customers

Consider the fact that most customers are looking for a specific product or service to solve a problem that exists in their lives and not just something random to spend their money on. You might be excited about specific features of your product or service, but the end result you should be trying to reach with it is the solution to your customer's problem. What is the specific problem that your brand can solve, and how can you solve it? As you learn more about what your customer is looking for, feel free to enhance what you are offering - what is missing from your product or service that can better help your customer?

More consumers than ever before are doing research on different brands and products before making their purchasing decision, and a positive first impression that stands out above the rest of the brands out there is crucial. Your solution to the customer's problem should be included at the beginning of your story and act as a cornerstone for the identity of your brand.

## Better Than Your Competitors

No matter what niche you are in, you should be better than each of your competitors in at least one area - otherwise, your target audience will have no reason to choose you over a different brand. Now is the part of the process where you identify your strengths and weaknesses. This can be done effectively with the help of a SWOT Analysis (using a SWOT template can be useful during this step).

Image courtesy of MindTools, SWOT Analysis worksheet template.

(https://www.mindtools.com/pages/article/newTMC_05.htm)

## Analyze the Competition

Part of beating your competitors to make the sale is knowing exactly what you are up against. Do some research and find out who your competitors are, both major and minor, to learn what they do and do not do well. One of the ways you can do this is by creating a spreadsheet where you can effectively compare your competitors to each other and your own brand to see their marketing efforts, quality of products or services they provide, reviews that their customers give them, and more.

After developing a good understanding of what each of your competitors' strengths and weaknesses are, take the time to answer a few questions. Is there consistency within other brands when it comes to marketing and the message they are sending out? How does the quality of competing products and services compare to your own? How does the public seem to feel about what your competitors are offering? What means are your competitors using for marketing that you should be taking advantage of?

Even if you like something specific that one of your competitors is doing, you should never imitate their exact approach - find a way to make it your own. Remember, you want to be different than your competition, and no one wants to be known as a copycat. Innovate the ideas that others have used and make them stand out within your brand.

## Identifying Your Idols

Ever since we were young, we had role models that we admired for different reasons (he is good at his job, she is a great athlete, they treat people well, etc.). Likewise, business owners have role models, or idols, that they look to for inspiration when creating their brands. Take some time to think about which brands you admired when you first started your business - what are some things that you borrowed from their methods that have worked well for you? What are some other brands that you should keep an eye on because they tend to have good ideas?

You might even realize that the values of your business were borrowed from one of your idol brands - and that is completely okay! You can have the same values as another company and still be seen as different from it as long as you make the products and services your own. Having the same values as another brand can be beneficial, as you can look to them for guidance on how to implement your shared values within your own brand.

## How Your Employees See Your Brand

Not only does a valuable brand positively impact what potential customers will think about your business, but it will influence your employees' perceptions as well. Do they have a firm grasp on the "why" of your business? Do their values align with those of your brand? Do they enjoy the work they are doing or are they just in it for the paycheck? In order to be a successful business, you will want to surround yourself with employees who feel strongly about what goals you are trying to achieve (this can be difficult if the work requires a lot of tedious tasks).

Remember, your employees are the hands and feet of your business - they spend a significant amount of time within its inner workings and can have some very insightful ideas on what your brand should look and sound like. Having a meeting with your employees to get a good understanding of how they see your brand is a great way to figure out what you should keep the same and what needs to change in order to have a good public image.

After having met with your employees and gathered some of their insights on what your brand means to them, look for the consistencies within their answers. What do they all seem to agree on? Does their take on the brand align with what you want it to be?

## Finding Your Brand's Voice

Finally, we are getting towards the end of the branding process! This is where all of your work gets put into action, and the voice of your brand is formed. Your brand's voice is essential for proper communication with those you are trying to connect with and sell your product or service to. The tone that you choose to use for your voice is particularly important - it needs to match your brand's identity and the values that you stand for. Your tone also needs to match your target audience - if you are selling gravestones to the bereaved, you should not use a comedic tone, for example. You want your customers to feel comfortable with you and feel good about approaching your brand.

Your brand's identity should remain authentic and consistent; these qualities allow your customers to become comfortable with you and trust your brand, and your employees to better understand the direction you want to take the business in.

## Build Your Message

Once you find it, use your voice to let the world know exactly who you are as a business. Let's look at *TOMS Shoes* as an example: one of the first things you see when you enter their website is the message, "Improving lives. With every product you purchase, TOMS will help a person in need. One for One." With these short, simple sentences, *TOMS* effectively lets the customer know what their values are and what they aim to do. Build your brand's message to tell your customers who you are and why they should care about what you do in a simple and easy-to-understand way.

Your logo will be the image that the public will identify with your brand, and it should encapsulate your business in a memorable way. In this step, you will likely benefit from the help of a professional designer to make sure that you end up with a result that you will be pleased with. This is also where you will develop your tagline - a quick phrase that will remind your customers of your brand and stick in their heads.

## Integrating Your Brand

The branding process will change as your business grows, but working on your brand will always be relevant as time goes on. Once you have established all of the details of your brand, you should start to integrate it into your outreach methods - if your customer sees, hears, or reads about your business, the brand you have created should be front and center. This means displaying your logo, tagline, and design schemes in your physical location and in your marketing methods (advertisements, business cards, packaging, etc.).

# *Stick With It*

Creating a brand requires commitment; you cannot change your brand shortly after creation unless you have discovered an important flaw. Be consistent with your brand and the representation of your business, including physical aspects, your voice and tone, and the guidelines you have set in place. Inconsistency can be dangerous - nothing will confuse your customers and employees more than inconsistency in your brand.

## Advocating Your Brand

Any employees that you hire should advocate your brand as well, so it is important to make sure that they fit within your brand's culture. Customers who have already used your product or service can do great things for building awareness of your brand - happy customers tend to share their experiences with others in their social circles. Allow your customers to leave reviews and share their opinions about your brand on your social media accounts and website so that the word will spread more quickly. Reviews and testimonials can also provide peace-of-mind for anyone who is browsing your site and considering giving your products or services a try.

Advertisements can only do so much to advance your brand. Your brand needs an advocate, and who better to advocate your brand than those who know it the best? **You** and those who understand the heart of your brand need to act as ambassadors, spreading the word about your brand and letting the world know what you have to offer. To get your employees involved, you can hold a meeting or send out a memo to share what you expect of them in regards to brand advocacy, as well as hear their ideas about how to be effective brand advocates.

## Beyond Definition

Knowing the finer details about what you want for your brand and how to get there is a vital part of the branding process. As you walk through the necessary steps, be sure to be patient and take your time so that you can be as thorough as possible and not overlook anything by mistake. Consulting with others before you reach the launching stage to gain some outsider insight can be a difficult part of the process, so be sure to take criticism with a positive attitude - do not only choose people who will be honest with you but those who will also present their opinions in a constructive manner.

And with that, you are ready to move forward and focus more closely on your audience and what you need to do to enhance your social media marketing experience!

# Chapter 2: Strategies for Your Audience

Your customers are one of the most important parts of your business - they might even be the most important factor of your business. Without customers, your business basically does not exist. Who are your customers, and how can you best reach them? Having a clear understanding of who your target audience is can help you to reach them efficiently and use your resources in the most productive way possible.

In Part 1, we talked about how your product or service should be catered to a specific audience from the beginning and how you probably already had a demographic in mind when you thought of the product or service you wanted to offer. But what if the target audience you should be going after is not as obvious?

## Defining Your Target

Narrowing down who your target audience will be is a vital part of any business - you cannot be everything to everyone, nor can you afford to be. Gearing your business towards a specific niche is the best way to start, as you perfect what you are already good at and provide for that niche. You can always expand your target audience after you have established a good following and built up more skills relating to your industry.

## Identify Your Customer Base

Who are your current customers? Which demographics are already flocking towards your products or services? Who are the people following you on your social media profiles, who like and share your content and actively engage with what you are putting out there? What do your current customers find appealing about what you are offering them? Which sub-categories within your customer base bring you the most business? Identifying who your current customers are can help you to expand slightly as you look for people who are similar to your customers who might also like what you are producing.

## Compare Your Opponents

Take a look at other businesses that are offering something similar to your products or services - who is buying from them? Are they different from your current customer base? If they are, what is it about your competitors' offering that appeals to them? Search the social media accounts of your competitors - what kind of content are they sharing, and how are their followers responding?

It might make sense to go after the same people as your competitors; after all, you want their business. But look beyond those who are buying from your competitors. Which niche are they overlooking that would be a prime target? How can you reach the ones being overlooked with your product or service?

## Analyze What You Are Offering

What is it about your products or services that appeals to those who are already buying from you? What are you offering on your social media accounts? Do your followers respond well, or could you use some more engagement on their part?

Think of the different features of your product or service and list the benefits that each of them brings to your customer. Who are the specific people who would enjoy these benefits? You can discover entirely new groups to target by examining your product or service.

# Demographics and Psychographics

With all of this information, consider now who you should be targeting as part of your audience. Broaden your search - who can benefit from what you are offering? Who are the people most likely to be interested? Think about age, gender, and occupation, as well as location, income and education levels, ethnic backgrounds, and marital/family status. Each of these demographics holds many different possible audience groups.

Psychographics, as well, should be taken into account when defining your perfect target audience. This includes the internal personal characteristics each person has, such as values, attitude, behaviors, and lifestyle. Think also about personality traits, hobbies, and interests. How would your product or service fit into your target's lifestyle? Which types of media (social or otherwise) do these groups first turn to for information or guidance? Which platforms are most likely to be successful in reaching these targets?

# Evaluate your decision

After analyzing all of these different areas, you should feel confident to make a decision about who your ideal target audience should be. Once the decision is made, act on and evaluate it. Ask yourself if your target audience will see the need for what you are offering them and if the price you are asking for it correlates with the demographics. How reachable is your target audience? Your message should be quick to grasp and easy to hold onto, both because of the message itself and the method you are using to convey it.

If you have different niches within your audience - and you should - consider whether or not the same message and method of delivery will work well to each niche. Having different demographics and psychographics within your target audience means reworking your message to accommodate different types of understanding; this is a good thing, as you do not want to set your gaze too narrow and only be able to reach a small number of people. You do not have to do all of the research you need yourself - there are plenty of people who have done this before you, so why not piggyback off of their research to reap the benefits?

Once you know who your target audience is, it becomes much easier to know which methods you should be using to reach them and get your product or service into the public eye. Use the platforms that most appeal to your target, and watch the awareness of your business spread!

## Reaching Your Audience

People in the marketing game make it seem so easy to reach out and get new clients. The truth is, it really can be easy - if you know how to get started. Catching people's attention can be done with different social media platforms, such as Facebook, Instagram,

Twitter, and the like. However, we are first going to take a look at the one that came before all of these options: email.

Why bother with email when we have all these other, more modern social media sites to use? With social media, you simply post your content and add tags to hopefully grab the attention of potential customers, whereas with email you are on the offense, sending your content directly to the consumer. Social media sites are great for keeping your audience updated and engaged, but email is the hook that brings them in to begin with.

Email is not just a great way to build your audience in the first place, but can also be one of the best options for keeping them engaged and coming back to take advantage of what you have to offer. 81% of shoppers in the United States are more likely to return to a store (either online or in person) because of promotional emails that they either signed up for or received based on previous purchases. Most of these shoppers also state that email is their preferred method of communication with their favorite companies, many of whom enjoy weekly or bi-weekly email promotions (reference 4). Clearly, email marketing is a significant lifeline of today's businesses.

## *Starting with the Right Software*

Maybe it sounds a little strange because of how simple email is to use, but there are different kinds of email marketing software options out there to help you get started. With the right software, things can become much easier, allowing you to automate your email list so that you barely have to lift a finger once the initial setup is complete.

Some options, like MailChimp, will offer a free trial or remain free up until you reach a certain number of contacts on your list, while others, like GetResponse or Remarkety, will have a monthly cost based on the number of contacts you have (i.e. fifteen dollars for one thousand contacts). When choosing the right software for your business, be sure to do some research first - you do not want to end up with software that will actually end up making things more complicated than they need to be. No matter which software you decide to go with, starting a Drip Campaign should be a part of its features.

# *Drip Campaign Marketing*

No matter how hands on you want to be in regards to consumer outreach, arguably the best way to go about growing your email list will be with a Drip Campaign, which sends designated content to the subscriber based on a timeline or user action. In a timeline campaign, a new subscriber will receive a new email every few days (depending on the business' preferences) without needing to take further action. The graphic below shows an example of an action-based campaign: the subscriber receives content based on his/her choice  Regardless of which type of campaign is used, each person who subscribes will receive the same content without missing important starter information.

# How to Build and Grow Your Email List

After picking your software, you are ready to get started building your email list. Be sure to steer clear of bad advice, like using business cards, telemarketing, and bombarding your friends and family about signing up - these methods will not work and will only lead to disappointment and frustration.

# A Content Strategy for the Long-Haul

Any big project needs a strategy to make sure that things move forward as planned and lead to the desired outcome, and your email marketing plan is no different. Create an outline for how often you want to release new content and put the plan to action. Creating new content regularly will keep your viewers interested and allow them to see that you mean to stick around and not leave them hanging. This content should be something that applies directly to your target audience. What is even better is creating relevant viral content consistently - you do not want to be a one-hit-wonder.

What constitutes viral content? What about your content will make people want to share it? Firstly, it has to be something that is quick and easy to read. You want to keep your grip on the viewer and stay within the average attention span (which is not very long). Keep your aesthetics pleasing with an easy-to-view color scheme, bold titles, and relevant graphics. Second, viewers are much more likely to share something if it makes them look smart and genuine for doing so. Keep it original, intelligent, and relevant.

Providing a way for the viewer to interact with your content and voice their opinion keeps them feeling involved instead of making them feel like an outsider ingesting information. Try using infographics, calculators, or quizzes to keep your viewers engaged and involved, and keep the content easy enough to comprehend so that they understand what they are forming an opinion on by reading your content.

# *Everyone Loves Giveaways*

Seriously, everyone likes to get things for free - what better way to draw in new subscribers than by giving them a free gift that has to do with your product or service? Creating multiple options (only two or three) to give your new subscribers as a reward is a good way to reach multiple people. We say "multiple" because not everyone will want the same thing; while one person would love your free ebook, another would rather have a video or some kind of product demonstration. Different personalities have different preferences, even within the same demographic. Providing options is a great way to get these different personalities interested in what you have to offer.

Giving out a coupon or discount can work great for pushing your product or service. After all, who does not like getting something for less than what it is worth? Everyone loves a good deal on something, even if it is not necessarily something they were planning on buying. Giving that discount gets attention and increases the likelihood of someone trying out what you are offering. If they like your product or service, they come back - it is as simple as that!

# Make Yourself Accessible

Remember, you are the one responsible for putting yourself out there. If you do not reach out to your target audience, how can you expect them to find you and become interested in you? Making your subscription form easy to find is key when trying to build your email list. For a traditional website, your signup form should be in two places: on your navigation bar and in your menu. Placing a link to your signup form right on your navigation bar keeps if front and center, reminding the viewer that they can have access to more of what they are here for with just a couple of clicks. Keeping pages in your menu that your target audience is specifically looking for and adding a link to your signup form somewhere on each of these pages can help to entice the viewer to want more of your content and encourage them to sign up.

For a blog website, you should add a signup form at the end of each of your blog posts. Afterall, if the viewer read all the way to the end of your post, they are obviously interested in what you are offering. You should also include the signup form on your About page, at the footer of your main page, at the top of the sidebar, and in the feature box, as these are all easy-to-see places that your viewers are likely to go to.

# *Your Initial Greeting*

Your first impression should be a positive, lasting impression. This means creating a friendly, inviting email response to any new subscriptions, which you will be able to do using your email marketing software. But what should you include in your initial email greeting? The following example is a great place to start:

*Hi* [Name of Subscriber]
*Thanks for joining our email list! My name is [your name], the [creator/founder] of [your business name]. As promised, here is the link to the free [product] you were looking for.*
*To get to know you better and how we can help you, we want to know what you are hoping to get from us, no matter how small. Feel free to shoot us an email to let us know!*
*Thanks again,*
*[your name]*

Inviting your subscriber to reach out to you and let you know what they are looking for helps them to know that you value them as a customer and are willing to do whatever you can to help them out. It also gives you a better picture of what your target audience wants or needs. Now you know what sort of content you can give them in the future to keep them coming back.

# Chapter 3: Getting Started with Social Media

Now that you know the finer details about what you want for your brand you can get started with creating and using social media accounts. Working with social media to launch your brand is based around interaction with consumers, which means focusing on your target audience. Consider which channels of social media your target audience uses most often and are more likely to feel comfortable using to interact with your brand. All social media channels are similar in certain ways, but they are still different and tend to cater to different demographics and psychographics. Picking the right channels to reach your target audience is an important first step in launching your social media accounts and campaigns.

## *Preparing for Launch*

Ultimately, what is the goal you are trying to achieve by using social media? Are you trying to raise awareness among people who have never heard of your brand before? Are you trying to encourage your current fans or followers to learn about a new product or service your brand is producing? The goal in mind should be specific, as should the demographic for your target audience.

Look into what is already happening among your target audience on social media: what are they talking about? What products and services are they looking for? What sort of information are they sharing with each other? Which questions are they looking for an answer to? Listen to what they are already saying without your brand introducing another topic to them.

Remember that human beings are creatures that respond to emotion; each demographic feels a certain way towards different things. Consider what emotions you can use to your advantage in reaching your target audience and getting the response you are hoping for. What inspires your audience? Which approach can you take to evoke a positive response? Should you use humor, vulnerability, sadness, etc.? Are they looking to be entertained or educated? With these questions in mind, look for a way to incorporate emotion by demonstrating what your product or service is capable of doing for the customer.

You also need to decide which types of content will be received the best by your target audience - videos, photos, articles, and more. When your audience receives your content, how will they respond? You want them to feel a call to action and see the necessity for your product or service. Take your time and do your research. Learn about your target audience so that you can better reach them and waste less time later on.

## Branding Strategies

The key to an effective execution is to have a good strategy - after all, you are fighting against countless competitors out there, and you cannot go about it without a game plan. Remember that you need to stand out, to shine amongst the other brands with products and services vying for the affection of your target audience. So, how are you going to make sure that your brand is well-represented?

# The Right Networks

Using the right networks for your outreach goals is crucial to the success of your brand's strategy; even the best brands would fail (or at least not be as successful as they should be) if the wrong social networking tools were being used instead of the right ones. Take a look around and determine which channels best suit your brand's image and work well for the categories that your brand and products/services fall under; you want any advertisements you use via social media to work well, too.

Try not to be tempted to use more platforms than necessary. There are so many options out there, and new ones are popping up all the time. You might think that having an account on every social media platform is the best way to boost awareness, but sometimes less is more. It is better to be good at a small number of things than to be alright at a big number, right? Having a smaller number of social media platforms to work with means having the time and energy to nurture them and maintain them properly. Success using social media to launch your brand takes effort.

We have already talked about doing some research to find out which channels your target audience uses most often and would be the most comfortable using to engage with your brand. After this is done, use the information to narrow down your best options.

Keep in mind that different types of media content work best on different social media platforms. That being said, ask yourself which types of content can effectively convey what you are trying to get across to your audience, as well as which types of content your brand produces well (but do not be afraid of trying new things and pushing your limits). The type of content you will create for your social media accounts will become a big part of your strategies.

## *Different Strategies for Different Phases*

You might only think of creating a strategy for the launch itself, but the time immediately before and immediately after your launch are also great opportunities to build your audience and get people excited about your brand. Sure, the launch itself should be the main event, but anticipation should not be underrated. Think about it: the film industry pumps out multiple movie trailers and teasers a year with the promise, "Coming Soon," knowing that the more people they reach with the teaser, the more people are aware of what they are about to release, and the more likely the theatres will be packed full. Without the initial announcement that your launch is coming soon, you lose a prime opportunity to build up hype and increase the number of potential customers.

The time after your launch is just as important - what good is a great initial launch if it is followed by something mediocre? Build a plan for after your social media accounts are launched and set yourself up for success before you are forced to make decisions about where to go next.

## The Face of Your Brand

Social media is largely visual. What this means is that creating visually appealing content is important if you want to keep your audience interested in what you are putting out there. Keeping the look of your different profiles consistent is the base of creating a visually appealing image for your brand and the products and services you are offering your audience. Consistency also allows your audience to easily recognize your brand regardless of which platform they see your content on.

How do you develop visual consistency? Start with an appealing **color palette** that you use in all of your graphics and content, from your logo to your advertisements. With enough exposure, you want your audience to associate these colors with your brand (whether they realize it or not). The best way to go about this is to look at your logo - what colors are present, and which of these are dominant? Stick with these and other colors that compliment your logo. When creating your color palette, remember that different colors have the ability to create different moods and might have a certain impact on how your audience feels about your brand.

Let's look at Coca-Cola as an example: if you go to their social media pages, there is a consistent feel across their Facebook, Instagram, and Twitter profiles. Their color scheme conforms to the style of their red and white logo, creating a consistent feel across the entire page and among their different platforms of choice.

As well as sticking to the same color scheme, you will also notice that Coca-Cola uses the same **logo** as their profile picture in each of their social media profiles. This is an excellent way to keep things consistent, and there is no quicker way to boost recognisability than to put your logo front and center. Of course, Coca-Cola has been around since the 1880s, so even many people outside their target audience will recognize their brand. But even newer viewers are able to recognize Coca-Cola soon after learning of the brand because their consistency makes them easy to remember.

Depending on which social media platforms you deal with, different **filters** are available to change the appearance of your content. While it can be fun to use these filters, you should try to stick to using the same filters for all of your content. Try picking no more than three different filters. Some platforms, like Instagram, will even let you save the filters that you use most or reorder them so that your favorites are placed at the front so that you can skip the search when you go to post something new.

If you are just starting out a small business, you will likely be handling social media yourself or have one person designated to do all of the social media work. Larger businesses, however, can find a social media team to be better when managing their online content. Using **templates** can make keeping the look of your profiles consistent easier. With the use of templates, anyone posting content to your social media profiles is guaranteed to have the right colors and styles to work with, and there is less of a chance of making a mistake. Photoshop (reference 8) and Canva (reference 9) are great tools for creating such templates.

## *The Voice of Your Brand*

The voice that you use to display your brand should be just as appealing to your target audience as the face of your brand. You want your voice - or the way you communicate with your audience -

to convey your brand's personality effectively, and finding that voice can take time. Eventually, your brand's voice should become clear and allow your audience to feel comfortable with your brand.

When trying to find the right voice for your brand, consider these three aspects: your business' culture, your target audience, and maintaining authenticity. The **culture** of your business consists of different characteristics, including language, habits, values, and more. So, ask yourself what the culture within your business is. What are your brand's highest values? What makes your brand different or special?

Effective communication with your target **audience** depends on mutual understanding. What sort of lingo is common among your target audience members? You want to connect with your audience, so you should be staying in tune with how they communicate and reach them on their level. You also want your audience to trust you and believe in the **authenticity** of your brand. Fitting in with your audience is great, but not if you have to sacrifice honesty to do so. Your brand's voice should feel genuine and align with what matters most within the business.

## *Maintaining Consistency*

The importance of consistency does not end with the visual part of your brand - the topics that are present in your content should all be relevant to the brand as well. **Topic consistency** can be aided by curating content from other sources, such as social media and relevant websites. Using curated content also brings variety to your social profiles and helps you to avoid getting stuck sending out strictly self-promotional information.

To make sure that you share curated content that aligns with your brand and does not cause confusion to your audience, you can follow topics that relate to your brand on social media. This way, content is placed right in front of you, and you can feel secure about relevance. Your audience follows you because of what your brand is about; you do not want to throw them off by sharing things that they do not care about.

You also want to make sure that your audience does not forget about you because you have not been **posting content regularly**. Sporadic behavior and unpredictability are unappealing characteristics for a brand to develop, and coming up with a schedule for when you should post new content can help to keep you consistent and reliable. The schedule you create will be dependant on the audience you are catering to, and you may have to play around with it a little bit before you really figure out what works best.

Using a scheduling tool such as Later (reference 10) or Sprout Social (reference 11) can make maintaining a posting schedule much easier than if you were to post your content manually. Tools like these can also use analytics to tell you when the best times to post content are, and which types of content get the most attention.

## *Making the Most of the "Bio" Section*

There is something unappealing about seeing an incomplete profile on social media, just like how seeing empty space on a resume gives a bad impression. Take advantage of every space that your chosen social media platforms offer, including the "bio" section of your profiles. This section is exactly where your audience will look to find out what your brand is about and what you do.

Large, well-known brands have the luxury of keeping the content in this section minimal (like including the brand's hashtag), but as a smaller business, you should be using this space to sum up your brand in a few sentences. Do not make the mistake of making a lengthy bio; this is a good way to lose the interest of the reader.

Just as you will use the same profile picture and color scheme for all of your profiles on different platforms, use the same bio for each platform.

# *Promotion & Engagement*

Once your profiles are completed, get some traction by **promoting** them heavily. No one will know about your social media profiles unless you share them, right? Put your profiles out there and invite others to share it as well. If you have business cards, brochures, or anything tangible that you use to reach your audience, include information about your social media profiles to help increase awareness.

You might also need to let those within your business know that you are on social media. A great way to do this is by using an employee engagement tool like Bambu (reference 12), where you can simply send out a message to everyone at once. You can also come up with a pre-written post for each of your employees to share on their own personal profiles as an act of promotion. Your employees are there for the company - use them!

The main uses for social media are to share and to engage with one another. Sharing content without engaging with others does not allow your social media accounts to live up to their full potential.

In the beginning when your brand has not yet gotten very much of a following, you can **engage** with others by commenting on relevant posts by other users and sharing your page and content there. You can even engage with competitors as long as it is kept respectful and playful. Engaging with your competitors can play to your benefit, as you make yourself known to their audience as well as your own.

## *Thinking Ahead*

We have already talked about sticking to a few social media platforms instead of jumping into all of them at once. We are not going to go back on that, but it is a good idea to reserve your place on other platforms for later, just in case you decide to give those platforms a try once your initial profiles are succeeding and you are comfortable branching out. Creating an account on other platforms is the best way to make sure that you achieve consistency across all platforms in the name you will be using.

Think about it: you want your name to be the same on every platform so that you are easier to find for your audience. If someone else uses your name before you have a chance to, they can change the reputation of your brand by the content they choose to share. You want your brand to be the first thing that shows up when someone uses Google to search for you, not someone else that has nothing to do with your brand.

## *Revamping Your Strategies*

Even if you have been using social media for your brand for a while now, you might not be getting the results you had hoped for, and it might be time to reevaluate how you go about your social media presence. Maybe you are not standing out quite as much as you were aiming for, or maybe your content just is not reaching your audience like you thought it would. These problems are nothing a little fine-tuning cannot fix.

## *Show Your Personality*

You spent a lot of time on creating a personality for your brand - social media is the place to let it shine! There are things that make your brand different from the others, and those differences are what will make a strong social media profile. You do not want to let the way your profiles function become robotic and lifeless. With the content you post, write your captions and comments in a way that blends with your target audience. Remind them why they follow you!

Social media is not just another way to advertise, but a platform for personal connection. So, let's get personal! It has been shown that story-driven posts and selfies are the types of content that do best on social media. Why? Because they are personal and people can relate to them. Try to make your posts sound less like a business and more like a friend, all the while showing your unique personality.

We all have different opinions, and it is definitely okay for them to be heard. Part of showing your brand's personality would include voicing your opinion. Keep in mind that this should be done with sensitivity and respectfulness kept in mind. Your opinion is part of what makes you stand out, especially if it is different than the majority of other opinions out there.

# Add Some "Pop" to Your Photos

Remember when we talked about making your profile visually appealing through color schemes and filters? The same concept can be applied to the content that you post. You want to be posting things that grab the viewer's attention as they scroll through their newsfeed. Get creative! Use colors and designs that pop out and make the viewer want to keep looking at it.

Like in the image above, eye-catching content can be used to highlight the brand and make their voice heard. Even if there are no photos that work for your product or service, you can add illustrations to an article or post to add a bit of "eye candy" for the viewer.

# Tags & Hashtags

**Tagging** or "mentioning" another social media user in one of your posts ensures that he or she will see your content, as well as putting it in front of the people that follow that user. This is virtually painless, as tagging someone only takes a second and requires no effort. Make sure that the content you are tagging them in is relevant though, otherwise, it can be considered spamming. You can also use **hashtags** to get the attention of anyone who follows those hashtags (again, relevancy is important here). Hashtags allow your content to be searchable, and you can even create your own hashtags for your brand or products and services.

## *Breaking News*

Originality is very popular these days, and that applies to what we see on social media as much as any other aspect of our lives. This can be useful if your brand is conducting original research on a topic, whether you are creating a new statistic, taking surveys, or conducting a case study. Why not break the news through your social media profiles? People love to be the first one to know something new, and providing that new information to your audience will give them something new to share and talk about with their followers and friends. It also allows you to contribute to the conversation in your niche instead of sharing old news time and time again.

## *Boosting Awareness*

Even if things are going well, there is nothing wrong with a little boost now and then. Here are a few ways you can give your viewer count a boost:

- Encourage your followers to share your posts, whether that means retweeting, repinning, or sharing to their profiles

- Create a contest that your followers can enter and/or gain extra entries by sharing your page or content

- Engage more with others by liking, sharing, and commenting on their content

- Create a post in which you ask your audience a question - this will show that you are interested in them, and not just because they like your product

- Share a video where you show your audience how your product or service works or customer testimonials

- Offer your viewers a free demo of your product so that they have the opportunity to try it out before making a commitment

All in all, you will probably have to experiment a little bit in order to get it right, but there is no reason why you should not be able to achieve the awareness you are aiming for when it comes to your brand. Just remember: you want to stick out and be different so that you do not blend in with everyone else. Let the uniqueness of your brand shine through the use of social media!

# Chapter 4: Creating a Strong Presence

The general use of social media is completely free to the public - this is perhaps the only feature that the public has been promised will not change by the makers and owners of social media platforms. Regardless of what type of account you set up - whether it be personal or business - your account will always be free of charge. What this means for you is that you have nothing to lose by using it to promote your business (unless you decide to use paid social media advertisements).

When you set up an account for your brand, you have the ability to set your target audience so that your posts will end up directly in front of who you want to see them. You will have to do some work, particularly in the beginning stages of growing your brand's following on social media, by means of being a good advocate for your brand and letting your current customers and the general public know that your brand is on social media. But when the initial groundwork is completed, your brand's social media page will naturally appear as suggestions for users who share interests with your current followers and fall into your set target audience's demographics. Social media provides you with the exact audience you are looking for, even if you decide to expand your target audience to different demographics.

## *Increasing Your Online Presence*

One of the main things you should be thinking about regarding your brand's social media profiles is how to increase your number of followers. The bigger your audience is, the more people will recognize your brand and the greater your chances of converting consumers to your brand. Brand recognition can lead to customer loyalty, which is exactly what you want for the wellbeing of your brand.

Even at the top of your game, there is always room for improvement with how you work with your audience. Always keep in mind who your audience is and how they are likely to change as time goes on. In the previous section, we talked about how to build up your social media profiles and use them to reach your target audience in the most effective ways possible. Next, we will take a look at the different platforms available to you and how to make the most of what they have to offer.

# Making the Most of Different Platforms

Among the most popular social media platforms as of January 2018 are Facebook, Youtube, Instagram, Pinterest, Snapchat, LinkedIn, Twitter, and WhatsApp (reference 15). We, however, are only going to focus on a few. Regardless of which platforms you choose to create an account with, you should try your best to gain a good understanding of how it functions and what your audience uses it for before you jump in and make a commitment. You can set up a personal account before creating one for your brand if you would like to take a look around and become comfortable with different features.

# Facebook

Facebook allows you to post a variety of content types, like photos, videos, articles, and links. Like we have already discussed, images are the best way to grab the attention of your audience as they scroll through their news feeds. That being said, images should be a regularly used type of media that you share with your followers. More than just for advertising purposes, you can post photos from live events that your business hosts or attends and encourage your followers to tag themselves or people they know. Doing this makes your photos visible to those who follow your followers and expands your audience.

Posting videos on Facebook is becoming more popular, as their effectiveness in reach is increasing. Creating a video specific to your target audience can be more difficult than creating an image, but it can also be worth the effort. Videos are more likely to go viral than photos, and viral content is the exact type of content that you need to help your reach explode.

You can use Facebook's Graph Search to find out which of your existing followers like different businesses and people by searching, "pages liked by people who like my page." This can increase the effectiveness of your marketing efforts if you target the audiences of those pages as well, as there is a chance that the shared interests of your followers can extend to others who like the same things as them. You can also use Facebook Groups to reach your customers in a different way, creating a group that relates to your industry to build closer relationships with your target audience.

# Instagram

The main feature on Instagram that grabs viewers and brings them to your content is the use of hashtags. On each post, you can add up to 30 hashtags that relate to the content of your post. Instagram users who follow these hashtags or who search for them will be able to see your content - if they like what they see, the will likely follow you.

It is important to not only rely on hashtags but also create an appropriate caption for your Instagram content. A well-crafted caption can help to increase the engagement of your followers. Captions should only be as long as necessary, considering how they are cut off from visibility after a few lines of text. Including a question in your caption encourages your viewers to engage even more, and inviting them to share your content with others increases your visibility.

A fairly recent addition to Instagram's features is the Story. Even though they are relatively new, hundreds of millions of people view them regularly. Roughly 1 in every 5 stories results in a direct message to the poster, and one-third of the stories that get the most views are posted by businesses (reference 17).

Regardless of whether you are using a regular post or the story feature, consider posting live content. Going live is a good way to grab the attention of your audience, and it encourages them to engage with your content as the post is happening. What is a good example of something you can make into a live post? You can go live when you attend a relevant event, receive a new shipment of your product, or even as your services are being used. Anything can be turned into content for your audience!

# *LinkedIn*

This platform is specifically meant to be used as a networking tool for businesses and professionals. A great way to spread awareness for your brand is to encourage your employees to include your brand on their personal profiles, along with their position within the business. This puts a link to your brand's page directly on the pages of your employees so that anyone who interacts with them and looks through their profile can see with whom they are affiliated and learn more by clicking on the link to your page.

You can search for and join different groups that relate to your brand's industry to grow your network, just like other social media platforms. Join in on the conversation within these groups to connect with other professionals in your industry and share your experiences. Sharing with other professionals increases trust in your brand, which in turn increases awareness and authentic followers of your business.

LinkedIn gives you the option of investing financially in your outreach strategy by promoting your page with advertisements and updates. The ads here target your audience by using different criteria like geography and industry to ensure that your content gets put in front of the right people to grow your viewer base.

## *Twitter*

Using Twitter is almost like attending a networking event from the comfort of your own home or place of business. You can chat with other professionals and put yourself on the radar of potential new followers by using hashtags and mentioning other users, much like Instagram and Facebook.

Twitter allows you to connect with businesses and news sources in your area, as well as those from farther away. If you make connections with local professionals, they are likely to share your content with their followers as you do the same with your own. Building relationships with others in your industry through Twitter is a great way to hear their stories and get some insight about what else you could be doing for your brand.

## *Tools You Should be Using:*

While using social media for your brand is generally straightforward, there are marketing tools out there specifically meant to make it even easier. These tools range from helping you schedule your posts to helping you figure out what content to post and when. They can help you to grow your followers to even greater numbers than by using social media alone.

# *Canva*

First off, Canva is not strictly just for social media. This website allows you to create templates, color schemes, graphics, and more for your brand - it is a particularly useful tool if you find that you have little time to create content for your social media profiles and little to no disposable income to hire someone to do it for you. With Canva, creating content can take a few minutes rather than an hour.

We have already talked about how important it is to include images with your content; Canva is where you can create those images to draw in your audience. From header images to infographics, Canva has a wide variety of templates to choose from depending on what sort of image you are looking to create and which platform you will be posting it on (you can even create your own templates or work without one altogether).

## Meet Edgar

If you take a look at some of the most popular brands in your industry, you might notice that their content is used more than once without losing its effect on the audience. This is part of what Meet Edgar does for you - it extends the lifespan of your content by resharing it at times when most of your audience is likely to see it. Edgar also takes a look at the demographics that respond to your content and matches them with more of your content based on category. Essentially, this tool works the same way as an ad would work, except you only have to share the content once and let Edgar do the rest.

This tool is perfect for anyone who is looking for someone else to do most of the work while they direct their efforts elsewhere. Meet Edgar works for different platforms, which means that all you need to do is sync your social media accounts to your Edgar account for your content to be seen everywhere.

## Buffer

Before you go out looking at different scheduling tools, take a look at Buffer. With this tool, you can put your marketing strategy on autopilot so that you are not spending hours a week posting content and checking in to see how it is working out. Buffer publishes your content for you depending on when your viewers are most active, allowing you to get the most out of your content.

## Feedly

This is a great tool to help with your curated content. With Feedly, you simply search for the people or brands that you would like to see news about and add them to your news feed. In the same way, as your social media feeds, Feedly's news feed will automatically be updated with posts by whoever you have decided to follow. This way, content for you to share as "curated" content comes right to you so that you do not have to go out searching for it.

Feedly allows you to highlight and make notes on anything that interests you so that you do not have to make any changes right away or forget your thoughts about the content. You can also sync your Feedly account with your Buffer account or share what you find directly to your social media profiles.

## Followers vs. Customers

Seeing a high number of followers on your social media profiles can be exciting, but remember that you want your hit count to mean something instead of just being a random number. After all, what is the point of having a large following if none of your followers actually buys your product or service? You do not want all of the work you have put into creating your brand and building up your strategy to be for nothing. So, how do you make sure that your followers are genuinely interested in your brand?

Adding the methods that we have already talked about to your marketing strategy is a good place to start, but there is more that you can do to make sure that your social media profiles are more than just a place to look at something pretty. As we have already discussed, get to know your audience before you put yourself out there. Taking the time to do the research before you launch your profiles will pay off in many ways, including the quality of follower you will attract.

Your audience is more likely to take your product or service seriously if they have a personal relationship with your brand. You can establish a relationship with your followers by responding to comments and direct messages in a friendly and timely manner. Really hone your customer service skills through social media to show your audience that you value their business.

Keep in mind that everyone loves a good deal. Think about how many people will buy something that they would not have considered buying before because it was on sale. Try offering a discount for your product or service or a small gift that is exclusive for your followers to get people to try your brand. If they like what they found, they will likely come back to pay full price later. Contests can work similarly to giveaways, exposing your brand to more people and encouraging your audience to get involved for a chance to win. That being said, you need to make sure that the prize you are giving away is worth whatever is required to enter the contest.

What you want is for your audience to be engaged by your content so that they will feel the need to be engaged with your brand by becoming a customer. Giving your audience the best online experience possible through your social media profiles will help them to see that your business is customer-oriented.

# Chapter 5: Rules of Social Media Marketing

Just like every other area of our lives, social media marketing comes with its own set of rules that should be followed if you want it to be done right and see success for your brand. Even though each social media platform has its own unique way of functioning, making your marketing strategy work through these platforms can be done by following the same general rules. In this section, we will take a look at these rules and how to best implement them for your brand to thrive on social media.

## The 5:3:2 Rule

One thing you will want to make sure of as you share content on your social media profiles is that you have a good balance of the different categories of content you are putting out there. This is where the 5:3:2 rule comes in: what you post should be fifty percent curated, thirty percent created, and twenty percent humanizing. This ratio has proven to be the most effective way to balance out your content to make sure that you are not just talking about your brand constantly. Your audience wants to know that you care about more than just yourself, and following the 5:3:2 rule is the best way to make that happen.

## Curation

Half of your posts should be curated content that is relevant to your brand's industry - that is 5 out of every 10. Looking around for curated content takes a bit of the pressure to create something original off of you and your team. It also helps you to stay up to date on what is happening in your industry outside of your brand. Sharing curated content will show your audience that you care about what is going on around you instead of only being focused on your own business, which is a good quality to have. By seeing your curated content, they will also see that you are not so caught up in your business that you are not aware of what else is happening.

We have discussed curated content in previous sections and its importance to your marketing strategy. Take advantage of the tools available to your business to make finding and creating curated content easier, like Feedly, Storify, Quora, and others.

## Creation

For every 10 posts you publish, 3 of them should be original creations. With these posts, you will want to sell your audience on your product or service. Try to avoid going hard here rather than using gentle suggestion to get your point across, as you do not want to push your audience away and see your followers leave. With created content, you can use different types of media, like infographics, videos, blogs, photos, and eBooks. Remember, variety is the spice of life and is more likely to keep your audience interested instead of showing them the same thing again and again.

# Humanization

The remaining 2 of your 10 posts should be content that shows the personal side of your brand. This is where you can add a sense of humor or creativity to your brand. Allow your audience to identify with your brand on a personal level by showing them that you care about more than taking their money or becoming the next big thing. This content does not even always have to be directly related to your niche - it can be completely random if that is what works best for you.

## Essentials of Social Media Marketing

There are some rules that are very specific to the platform you are using, while others are general and can cover multiple platforms. The rules we will go through here can be followed for such sites as Facebook, SnapChat, Instagram, Pinterest, LinkedIn, and Google+. Regardless of the platform, the general rule that comes before all of the rest is that your audience and remaining personal is key. Social media is about engaging with people on a personal level, and marketing is not exempt from this fact.

# Rule #1: Make a Plan

Just in case we have not done enough to drill this home yet, we will say it again: make sure that you **have a plan before you start to act**. Create an outline, do your research, and construct a detailed plan to make sure that you are headed down the right path for what you are hoping to achieve for your brand. You need to have a clear vision for what you are about to do if you want to be met with success.

What should you include in this plan? Right from the start, you need to know the values behind your brand, the important qualities of your product or service, and who you are going to try to reach with your brand's message. Know who you are and why you are doing what you are doing before you turn to focus on your product, and know your product forwards and backwards before you move on to focus on your audience. There is a method to the madness here, so try to fight the urge to rush through it to get to the end. Having structure when executing your plan is important and you do not want it to crumble because you overlooked something.

# Rule #2: Build a Strong Foundation

When we talk about building a strong foundation, we are talking about creating **strong social media profiles** to start your brand's outreach. Following the information that we have already covered in the previous sections should help you to build up profiles on whichever platforms you choose to go with. Start by filling out the different sections that each platform outlines for you on your profiles and making sure the information you give is clear and uses words that accurately portray your brand while grabbing the reader's attention. Do not leave any spaces blank as you fill out your profile. Include your logo and your brand's tagline if you have one.

You want your profiles to look professional and creative while **showing your brand's personality** and adding personal touches to show your target audience that you are the right brand for them. Make sure to use the first-person narrative when writing in your information, as this helps to make things sound more personal and less robotic or generic. Use keywords when creating descriptions if you are using Twitter, Pinterest, or Instagram so that you do not fill up the small amount of character space with unnecessary fillers. For platforms like Facebook and LinkedIn, you have a bit more space to talk about who you are, but you should still keep things short and sweet so that your readers will stay interested in what you are saying instead of giving up a few lines in.

Facebook, LinkedIn, and Google+ have the option of creating a **business page**, which is no less important than your profile. You can use this page to provide updates and promotions about your brand to your followers, and share links that lead to your other profiles and websites. This is also a good place to share information about any job openings you might have or start conversations with your followers. In order for the business page to be useful, you need to maintain it, updating regularly and paying attention to any comments or messages that come your way through it.

# *Rule #3: Connect with Your Peers*

Just because other brands and businesses are technically your competition, you can still gain something from **connecting with them as peers**. Social media is the perfect place for networking and making contact with like-minded individuals. Building healthy relationships with others in your industry can greatly benefit your brand as you share tips and experiences with one another as you grow your business and grow your fanbase.

Developing relationships with other brands opens the door to opportunities to **collaborate** with each other, which can do great things for your follower list as you make yourself available to the audience of your collaborators and vice versa. You might also benefit from a mentor-mentee relationship if you reach out to big influencers within your niche. Engaging with competitors in a playful, respectful way through comments and shared posts allows your audience to see that you are not hostile towards other businesses, making you more likable by consumers.

Joining **communities and groups** that relate to your industry opens up the doors to more shared content that you can use, and responding to threads by other users shows your interest in things other than your own brand. When looking for groups to join, look for ones that already have people in them that belong to your target audience - getting involved in groups like this and sharing your content when it is relevant to do so shows these potential followers what you are offering without going directly to them and looking like you are only interested in self-promotion. You can also be a part of **promotional groups** that are specifically meant for sharing content to get promotion from other users and collaborate with others.

# *Rule #4: Publish Effective Content*

We have gone over the different types of content you can post on your social media profiles to pique the interest of your followers in the other sections, so we will not dwell too heavily on it here. As we have already said, **visual content** is the most popular content that will get your audience's attention the easiest. This could be in the form of photos, videos, gifs, infographics, or other images, as long as it relates to your brand or industry.

Whichever type of content you are using, make sure that it is **visually agreeable**; you want to use colors that appeal to the eye and evoke a certain feeling to the viewer. You can use social media tools (as we have already mentioned) to create images with templates and color schemes, such as Canva or Photoshop depending on your preference and experience creating graphics. If you are using an image for a header or title of an article and will be sharing it on different platforms, be sure to use the same image for each platform so that there is a continuous feel for the piece.

You want to provide content that reaches each type of person within your target audience, so do not be afraid to shake things up by sharing a **variety** of topics that appeal to the different demographics that your brand is catering to. In order to give the best possible experience for your followers, you need to understand what is important to them, how they think in general, and how they feel about key concepts. What does your audience respond positively or negatively to, whether that means a type of content, platform preference, or topic?

Keep in mind that different types of content will work better on some platforms than others. You can customize the same content to work nicely on each of your profiles so that no matter which platform your audience is using, you are still getting your message across to them. When adding **keywords**, **hashtags**, and **mentions** on your posts, make sure to use the ones that fit best with the content so that the right people will be directed to your content.

You can share content that you know is already **popular** if you are stuck for something to post. This way, you know you will get a positive response, and in the chance that some of your followers have not already seen it elsewhere, they will come to you first next time because you have already delivered in the past.

# Rule #5: Connect with Your Audience

Your audience is the lifeblood of your brand - you do not want to make the mistake of taking them for granted or neglecting them. As your audience comments on your content, make sure that your responses consist of something more than, "that sounds cool," or, "thanks for sharing." **Respond** with questions or personal anecdotes so that your responses have meaning behind them. Responding to comments, questions, and private messages shows that you are willing to actively participate with your followers and want to be in relationship with them. It gives a more personal touch to your brand, which is part of what keeps your followers around.

If you have a specific person in charge of handling social media (or if that person is you), make sure he or she is spending sufficient time per day **interacting** with your brand's audience and provides timely responses to all questions, comments, and concerns that come your way. Your audience needs to know that support is available to them when they need it - no one wants to wait a week to get an answer. In your responses, make sure you are being polite and helpful rather than rude or "salesy." People asking questions are more likely to respond positively if you greet them in a friendly manner.

You can create **communities and groups** within your page for your followers to join based on different topics relating to your brand. These places are great for smaller, more in-depth discussions to get involved with.

# Rule #6: Provide Incentives

Sometimes your audience might need a little bit of a push to take a chance on your product or service - and that is completely normal. You can offer **incentives** to show your audience that you have faith in your brand and what you have to offer, which in turn helps them to feel comfortable taking a chance on your brand. You can offer exclusive incentives that are only available to followers on specific channels to increase traffic to those platforms, and you can even make offers that will appeal specifically to certain niches within your audience at different times (after all, it is always exciting when something comes along that is specifically for you, is it not?). Limited-time offers create a sense of urgency to take advantage of whatever it is you are offering, which can also boost traffic during that time period.

# Rule #7: Be Generous

**Generosity** is a good way to increase your brand's popularity among social media users. Being generous can be done in a number of different ways depending on the platform you are using. On Facebook, it could mean sharing posts by non-profits with your friends and followers. On SnapChat, it could mean sharing stories that authentically represent your brand's values to spread the word about what can be done to inspire good in others. On LinkedIn, it could mean giving a recommendation or endorsement to another user to help boost their profile.

Being kind and generous to others on social media can have a great positive impact on those who are following you, as they see that there is more to your brand than self-preservation and "looking out for number one." We should all do our part to help make a difference in the world, no matter how big or small, and trying to make a difference through your brand instead of your own personal image helps to humanize your business. Humanization helps to build trust between you and your audience, and it can be done with little to no effort or sacrifice to yourself.

# Rule #8: Expand Your Reach

Once you have settled into your strategy and things are running smoothly, you can work towards expanding your reach and using different platforms more effectively. A good way to make sure that your audience has access to everything you are releasing is to **connect your social media channels** and any other platforms you are using, like blogs or websites. You can use one channel to promote the others with graphics and demonstrational videos to get your audience interested in what else you have out there. This can work for promoting your brand in general as well. Say you have a promotion available on SnapChat - use your Facebook and Instagram profiles to promote your SnapChat profile. Your followers will know that since SnapChat only has content available for a certain amount of time, they will have to act fast to get your offer.

If you have a website created through a platform like WordPress, you can include **social media buttons** to link all of your social media profiles to your main website - your website acts as an anchor where all of your profiles come together. With one click of these buttons, your viewers are able to access each of your different profiles to reach your content.

Although social media is free to use, you can always give your publicity a boost with the use of paid **promotions** and **advertisements** without pouring too much money into it. By paying a small fee, the platform you have chosen will show your advertisement to social media users outside of your followers based on the demographics of your target audience. Ads and promotions generate more traffic for your profile or page, and the odds of picking up more followers is increased due to the platform's advertising methods.

# Rule #9: Analyze and Adjust Your Strategy

Every social media platform comes with its own **analytics** tool to help you keep track of what does and does not seem to be working for your marketing strategy. For example, Facebook has Facebook Insights to track your page or profile traffic and engagement information, and LinkedIn has Company Page Analytics to see your statistics. With the analytics tools provided, you can see which demographics respond to your different types of content so that you can change your methods to better reach your target audience. You can also keep track of what content does best at which time of day and on which platforms.

These tools do all of the heavy lifting and leave you with one job: making a decision on what to change and what to leave the same. You need to give your profiles a fair amount of time before making any judgments, so try out your strategies and track the data for a period of 3 to 6 months at a time. Remember that different strategies will work for different demographics and platforms, and be patient when trying something new. Getting your marketing strategy just right will take time, but your patience will pay off once you have gotten it just right.

# Chapter 6: Tactics for Building and Growing Your Audience:

## *Starting a Like Campaign on Facebook:*

If you plan to make use of Facebook at all, you'll want to start by creating a page for your brand. Even if the brand is YOU, you should still create a separate page for yourself. Pages work differently and are formatted differently from personal Facebook profiles. One of the biggest differentiators is "likes." You can't get likes on your personal profile, but you can get as many likes as you want for your brand/company page.

As much as people hate to admit it, they're heavily influenced by the amount of likes something has on facebook. When they see that something is exceedingly popular, they will be intrigued. They will think, this must be important enough to pay attention to. That's how videos go viral on facebook and youtube. Once you get 10's of thousands of views on your video, people that aren't even actively interested in the topic of the video will likely watch it just to see what it's about and how it garnered so many views. This may or may not hold their interest.

Similarly, with brands, people are more trusting and interested in brands that have a big presence. If you're selling T-shirts and you have a facebook page that's linked to your website, people will pay a lot more attention to your page if you have a lot of likes. I'm talking 5,000+. People are wary of brands that don't seem to be popular or don't have much of a social media platform. They think these brands are unreliable or irrelevant.

You might be thinking, that's fine, but how am I going to get to 5000 likes. There a lot of ways to go about this. As with any marketing effort, the harder you work, the more results you'll see. However, for many people, when launching a brand, they may find it effective to create a like campaign. This is a paid advertising technique through Facebook where you advertise through content and paid ads to encourage likes on your page. This can be an extremely effective technique for people who are just starting out and don't have much of a following.

Once you've built up a solid amount of likes, not only will your brand be more credible, but you'll be able to market directly to people who've liked your page and also to their friends. On Facebook, you may often see content in your news feed from a brand's page that you haven't liked yourself. Then you'll see in the notes that several of your friends have liked this brand and that's why it's showing up in your feed in case you also find it interesting.

Using Facebook pixel and Facebooks incredible tools to target a highly specialized audience, you will be able to maximize your ROI and reach people that are most likely to engage with your brand.

For an effective campaign, you'll want to set a goal and a budget as well as a strategy. Here is an example that might help.

Goal: You want to get your T-shirt page from 0-5,000 likes in two weeks.

Budget: You're not sure how much it will cost so you have to experiment for a few days with different settings to see how much these ads will cost you. Once you've fine-tuned it and identified the most effective settings, you can see that a like will average out to about 10-12 cents. Thus, your budget should be about $600 (a small price to pay for the potential payoff).

Strategy: Through split testing and experimenting, you've found the optimal audience and the optimal keywords. You will then strategize how your budget will be spent. You'll set a bidding strategy (it's usually most effective to set automatic bidding so Facebook can optimize it for you), and just set a maximum spend per day. While you're in the testing and tweaking phases, you'll want to set a small budget (less than $15 per day) and once you start getting a feel for what works best, you can increase your budget and launch your two-week like campaign.

Although there are many guides out there to help you get the best ROI for your Facebook advertising campaigns, you have to remember that many of the factors will depend on your brand and desired audience. Therefore, the most effective strategy is often to test out different keywords and demographics and content until you find one that'd delivering the best ROI.


## Getting Followers on Instagram:

When just starting out, it can seem so overwhelming. You see so many profiles—people with 10's of thousands of followers and you feel like you won't be able to compete with that. Although building a following takes time and effort, you can quickly exponentially grow your audience both organically and with paid strategy.

You should know that many Instagrammers have "bought" some or all of their followers. There is a huge market out there for buying likes, followers and engagement. This practice is not just restricted to Instagram either, you will find it on Facebook, Twitter, and Youtube as well. Although some people might find this practice distasteful, it can be one of the quickest ways to establish an audience. However, many would argue that your audience won't be very engaged with your brand since you purchased them instead of winning them by attracting and engaging them. It is legal and can help to generate hype around new brands. If you're put off by this idea, you should know that many of your competitors are following this practice and it will be difficult to compete with them.

There are other ways.

**Join Instagram Engagement Groups:** Finding groups (especially on Facebook) can be a great way to find people interested in your niche. By contributing meaningful content and engaging actively in the group, you will become a valued member and will be able to glean followers from the group—especially from people who have shared interests. It is important to be generous with who you follow as well. Make sure you are also engaging with new members and helping them with their own pages.

**Getting Featured:** Getting someone else to feature one of your posts or to tag you in their post can go a long way. It will drive traffic and interest to your profile. Of course, similarly, you must be willing to do the same for others. You'll want to be careful with who you feature—their image and message should be relevant to your audience. It should be presented in such a way as something your audience would want to hear—and not just sales pitch.

**Consistency:** being consistent with your posts and style will attract attention. If people start to know what to expect from you, and it aligns with their interests, they will likely become a follower. However, if your posts are sporadic and all over the board and don't flow, people won't really understand your brand or your influence and won't be drawn to you. Although it may be tempting to post a wide variety of things and focus on a wide variety of content to reach people of many different interests, you will get lost in the crowd. You want to focus on your niche and do it as well as you can as consistently as possible.

**Get Influencers:** whatever your brand is—whatever your product or service, you need customers. The truth is, people want to hear from your customers. Sometimes, they want to hear from your customers even more than they want to hear from you. They want to hear from a real consumer—someone just like them who has used your brand and has something to say about it. Why do you think people pay so much attention to reviews of products and testimonials? If you can get a few of your best customers to give you a shout-out on Instagram or Facebook or Twitter, or tag you or your brand in their relevant post, you will strengthen your brand and encourage more people to follow you and to engage with your brand.

**Follow and Engage with Fans of Your Competitors:** many people win followers this way. By identifying who your competitors are, you'll be able to identify people who are actively engaged with them. By following them and engaging with them, they'll often return the favor by following you back or engaging with your brand. On Facebook and Twitter especially, reposting and retweeting the content of influencers and/or questions of people you hope to win over is a great way to boost engagement and increase your followers.

**Sharing Awesome Content:** This might seem obvious, but many people fail to do this. When sharing content, it shouldn't be all self-promotion. In fact, only a small portion of the content you share should be self-promotion. Especially in the beginning, your audience or potential audience will be wary of you. They haven't become established fans of you and your brand yet. You really want to focus on content that they will find informative, entertaining or at the very least relevant to them. In Digital Marketing, they talk about the 70/20/10 Rule for content marketing. 70% of the time, you should be sharing content that adds value to your audience's lives while simultaneously strengthening and building your brand. 20% of what you post should be others' content. This content can be complementary to your brand or else promoting someone else's brand that doesn't directly compete with yours. As with everything you post, it should be geared towards adding value to the lives of your customers. Keep your sales pitches to an absolute minimum—this is not the time for the hard sell. Content sharing on social media is all about becoming relevant and becoming a valuable contributor. The remaining 10% of what you post can be self-promotional as long as its constructive. This 10% can be strategically sprinkled in amount the other 90% so that people are aware of and interested in your brand's offering, but are not feeling like they're being sold to.

## Rapidly Increasing Your YouTube Subscriptions:

There are many people advertising tricks and hacks to get thousands of YouTube subscribers. Most of them are spammy and will get your account banned, but the few that may work in the short-run most likely won't achieve the desired effect. As with most social media marketing efforts, you have to keep your sights always set on the real goal. Your goal isn't just to have a lot of subscribers, your goal is to have a lot of customers. Or even a medium number of very devoted customers. People often mix this up. They opt for the quickest easiest way to a large amount of subscribers, but find diminishing returns. You could get more engagement from 500 true fans, than 10,000 spammy subscribers that you purchased. If you're trying to increase your following and become a social media powerhouse, your goal with youtube should be engagement, views, and growing your fan base. If you have a bunch of "fake" subscribers, or people who aren't actually interested in your brand but whose subscription was purchased, you likely wont get that many views on your videos from your subscribers. A true subscriber will want to watch every video you put out, many of them will like the videos and some will even share them on their personal social media accounts. This is why it's important to establish a true fan base. With YouTube, starting small and growing little by little has proven again and again to be the best way to grow.

**Start with People You Already have access to:** Promote, promote and promote some more. Encourage everyone you know to share and promote your videos. Make them feel like they are brand ambassadors and part of the movement. You can do giveaways and grand prize drawings and have people share your video to qualify.

Promoting is not enough however. Your video has to be quality. Your message has to be important and relevant to the audience you're trying to reach. If you can find ways to reach this audience where they hang out, you will have better success. Get involved in the conversation. Are there Facebook groups? Web Forums? Reddit conversations? Think of any resource you can find where people are having conversations similar to yours and think of creative ways to get them excited about what you have to say. Find ways to get them involved. Make them feel important and part of the discussion. Do not be self-centered and always a self-promoter. You need to show them that you want to provide value to the group as a whole—not just people you know.

**The Title is Important:** Make your titles searchable. Find the most compelling keywords that apply to your brand and video topic, and put them in your title if at all possible. Be careful because you want your title to be eye-catching and unique without seeming like clickbait or spam. If you cram too many keywords into your title, people will be suspicious and your video may be flagged or removed. Using Google Keyword Planner and websites like BuzzSumo will help you find the most popular keywords in your niche. This may also help you determine trend-worthy topics for your videos and channels if you ever need help with coming up with topics to talk about.  You'll want to keep your video under 50 Characters if possible since Youtube will automatically shorten your title for search results anyway.

Customize the Video Thumbnail: Create an image for the Video that creates interest and gives a preview of what the viewer will get once they click on the video. Using large, easy to read text over the image will also help quickly explain to the viewer what they're looking at.

## *Building Your Audience on Twitter:*

**Get a Professional and Eye-Catching Profile Picture:** if you are a brand and not necessarily associated with one person, you can make your profile picture your logo or something related to your brand. If you are your brand, then you'll want a great, eye-catching photo of you. People like to know who they're dealing with and since Twitter is quite different than Facebook and Instagram in that it's not full of photos of you, this might be one of the few places on twitter where they can see what you or your brand looks like. Under your profile photo, put a statement that says what you want to say about your brand. Include a link to your website, a hashtag if you have one etc. This is where you can differentiate your brand and show people what you stand for in just a few short words.

**Be Responsive:** By far the best thing you can do to increase your fanbase on twitter is to be responsive. Luckily, this is also the most straight-forward strategy you can employ. Any time anyone tweets at your brand, tags you, uses your hashtag, dm's you etc. respond as quickly as you can. This shows that you care about their interest and that you're there for them. This is an age of instant gratification. People don't want to wait for a response. Often whoever responds quickest gets their business. People want to know that they're dealing with a consistent, efficient and professional brand—this is where you can show them that you are all of those things. Many people make the mistake of taking tweets personally. If someone tweets something negative about your brand or something you don't like, this is not a chance for you to start a twitter war. This is also not a chance for you to make excuses or discredit the complainant. This is your opportunity to take the high road and show everyone how professional your brand is. Address the complaint no matter how rudely it is phrased. Apologize no matter whose fault it is. If there's an opportunity for you to make it up to the unhappy customer or follower, offer it to them. The worst thing you can do here is to make excuses or to argue back. No matter what people might think about the complaint, they will be impressed when they see your professional response. They will think of you as a real brand that cares about their customers and will take care of them. It builds trust in the brand.

**Tweet A Lot:** this is completely different than Youtube and Facebook and even Instagram. Twitter is all about short frequent messages and content. Posting once a week on twitter wont get you anywhere. Even once a day is not enough. An optimal number of tweets is 15 per day. The good news is that you can automate much of that. Each day or even each week, you can set up all the tweets for the day then schedule them all out so that you don't have to even think about it day to day. That's not to say that you don't have to go on twitter regularly. You should be as responsive as possible to interactions with your followers. The more you post, and the higher the quality of the content you post, the more followers you will get which will lead to more interaction with and interest in your brand.

**Pin Your Best Tweets:** A tweet that gets a lot of likes and/or retweets that you feel contributes to the strength of your brand can be a great tweet to feature at the top of your feed as a Pinned Tweet. It will catch the attention of newcomers when they see how many likes and retweets you got, and it will also give them an idea of what type of content you curate. This will make them more likely to follow you. Be careful not to pin too many posts and change your pinned posts from time to time. As with al social media, you want to avoid being spammy or gimmicky at all times. Savvy consumers can see right through that and will give you a wide berth.

# Chapter 7: Social Media Engagement

While we have talked about building your fanbase and putting your brand's best foot forward on social media, it is important to note that your goal should probably not be to become famous. There are so many celebrities out there, from actors and actresses to reality television stars to Youtube sensations, and achieving attention to the extent of fame is easier than it ever has been before. Even so, trying to achieve fame for your brand can be harder than it looks.

Here is a question to consider: is it better to have millions of followers or a thousand true fans? Followers will like or share your content if it catches their eye, but a true follower will seek out your content and commit to buying your products or services. An article on The Technium (reference 21) defines a true fan as, "a fan that will buy anything you produce," and states that in order to make one hundred thousand dollars per year, you only need one thousand true fans. The idea here is that you would need to make a profit of one hundred dollars per fan (so, one hundred dollars after any fees that it costs you to produce your product or service).

In order to keep true fans, you need to develop a relationship with each and every one of them; learn their names and which products interest them the most, what it is they love about what you are producing, and what they care about in general. Show your fans that you care about them and what they like, and they will be sure to stick around and commit to your brand. You do not need to be famous to be successful - you just need to find your true fans and connect with them.

## *Finding Your True Fans*

Considering the number of people in the world with access to the world wide web, it might be hard to find which of these people will be fans of your work. For all you know, the people that would love to see your content the most live in parts of the world that you are not necessarily targeting through the setup of your social media platforms. There is not a quick and easy way to locate your biggest fans before they know that you exist, unfortunately. Instead of going out and looking for true fans, let them come to you while you do what you can to create relationships with your audience. Of course, there are ways that you can create true fans out of the followers you already have.

If we have not already said it enough, the way to keep your viewers around is to engage with them through commenting and messaging and by creating interesting and interactive content - this takes much more than simply asking someone to "like" your Facebook page. Take a look at the following acronym (reference 23) to get some ideas about successfully engaging your audience.

## *Ask Questions*

Asking a question is arguably the best way to get a conversation going, but you will want to make sure that the questions you are asking are not conversation stoppers. For example, simply asking someone their name or how they are can only be met with a few short answers. Try asking a question that your audience will want to give details on, like, "What do you think about this?" At least fifty percent of the time, people who spend time online are there to give their opinion on something. Everyone has an opinion, so asking what your audience thinks about an issue or something you have posted is an easy way to get them involved. If you want to get more specific with your questions, go for it!

If you have an email list or are sending out group messages to your audience, ask them for a response. Most emails that you get from businesses specifically say not to respond to the email, but how often do you get one that encourages a response? If that is not enough, try making it a little more personal by specifically saying, "respond to **my** email," instead of, "respond to **our/this** email." Using "my" here humanizes your brand and encourages engagement even more.

You can also ask questions in the form of a poll or trivia game. You can easily create polls on different social media platforms that will make your audience feel involved while at the same time giving you a deeper look at what they think. Trivia questions and personality quizzes have worked for a long time in getting followers to stick around, so why not give them a try?

## *Encourage Expression*

The content that you post is the way you express your brand's personality, so why not encourage expression in your followers as well? Asking the audience to get creative in their responses to your content is a unique way to get to know them and allow them to express themselves, which you do not see everywhere else. You use all sorts of different features to express yourself through your content, like stickers, emojis, audio, filters, and more, so give your audience the chance to do the same.

One way you can do this is through media upload contests, where viewers can create and share their favorite meme, take a unique photo, make a video of their own, or something similar. This can work for drawing/painting, recording audio and video, writing prose, or any sort of creative outlet that can relate to your brand.

A number of social media platforms allow the use of hashtags, so why not encourage expression through this tool? Inviting your audience to add their own hashtags to your content gives them a say and allows them to express what they think of what you are posting. You can also ask for reviews or testimonials of your brand's products or services to let your audience verbally express what they feel about your brand.

## Provide Incentives

Including an incentive on your promotions is a great way to appeal to the competitive side of your audience. You can offer prizes of different sizes or introduce games where the score leads to some sort of bonus. People love games and the opportunity to win something of value, and if including an incentive is going to increase the loyalty of your audience, then it is a win-win for you and your viewers. Make sure when coming up with your incentive that it is something of interest to your target audience that they will actually want to participate for.

## Make Offers

Coupons, discounts, membership perks, free shipping, and other offers give your audience a reason to want to sign up to be a regular customer instead of a casual viewer. Different demographics within your audience will want different offers, so play around with which types work best for your following and continue with which ones work the best.

Facebook is particularly good at helping with offer promotion. With Facebook's **offer ads**, your customers can redeem your offer either in-store or online. Make the most of these ads by offering a substantial discount of at least 20 percent, using a set timeframe for the ad to run its course (7 days is an ideal length of time), using an image that will capture the attention of anyone who sees it, and pinning the ad to the top of your page while it runs so that anyone who visits will see it first thing.

# Deliver Utility

Along with engaging your audience, the whole point of having interactive content on your social media profiles is to educate the audience. Providing utilities that your target audience can make use of is both helpful and practical. You can use blog posts, infographics, photos, videos, mini-courses, webinars, and other tools to help your viewers and show that you are there for them when they need it.

## Exceeding Expectations

Because of its convenience to the user and how quickly things move, social media is easily the most preferred channel by customers when it comes to getting in contact with brands. Consumers have come to expect a certain quality of service, no matter which brands they are dealing with, and will look elsewhere for their needs to be filled if service standards are not up to par.

For example, the majority of consumers that use social media to contact their preferred brands expect to receive a response to their inquiries within four hours of sending them in. In reality, the average response time is about ten hours. Imagine the response of your audience if you not only managed to beat the average but also exceed their expectations for your brand? While it is not possible to track hypotheticals, you can use analytical tools on social media to keep track of different statistics that will let you know which areas you need to improve and the engagement patterns of your audience. We will talk more about analytical tools in the next section.

# *Build a Strong Team*

It might only be you when you first launch your brand, but as things grow and needs become more apparent, you will likely need to build a social media team to make sure that all the bases are covered. Having a strong team of social media experts can help you avoid having customers fall through the cracks and feel like they are not being heard or valued. It can also make the process smoother and less stressful for everyone involved.

There are five different categories to break your social media team into: content creators, community managers, public relations, sales and enablement, and support. Depending on the size and demands of your audience you can group a couple of these together. Your **content creators** are the ones making content to be posted, as well as publishing posts, coming up with ideas, and handling the scheduling tools. **Community managers** will be there to handle big news items and controlling any complicated situations that might arise. Your **public relations** manager's job is to create exposure for your brand and take care of a customer, client, and business relations. Your **sales and enablement** team provides information to customers about your brand and any products or services you offer, as well as promote engagement with anyone who might be interested in your brand. Finally, you need customer **support** to receive any complaints and put out fires as they come up.

# Becoming an Engagement Expert

As your brand goes through different stages of its lifespan, always remember the important role that your audience plays. You are bound to face different phases of varying difficulties and find different methods when it comes to content creation or marketing strategies that you will want to try. Do not worry - there is absolutely nothing wrong with that.

Regardless of where you find yourself, engage your audience and work towards meeting the needs of your true fans. Your true fans will be the ones that you can depend on to an extent and that you can base a portion of your strategies around. As the phases that your true fans go through will change, so must you change things about how you relate to and communicate with them.

# Chapter 8: Using Analytics to Maximize Efficiency and Guarantee the Biggest ROI

Arguably, there is not much of a point to putting in all this effort if you are not going to keep track of the finer details of your social media marketing strategy. Those details can help you to know exactly what is or is not working for you and what you need to do to make things work better. Every social media platform should come with its own in-house analytics tool built right into the site itself for your convenience. Even if these in-house tools did not exist, there are plenty of other sites that are completely independent of the various social media platforms that can help you to analyze the performance of your marketing efforts and determine the changes that need to be made. How should you be using these tools, and why would you spend your valuable time looking at marketing data when you could be spending it on more important things?

## Using Analytics

Any analytical tool that you might use will collect information about your followers, like what they respond to, when they respond most often, and whether their response is positive or negative. Paying attention to this and other information collected can help to guide your marketing strategy to its most effective state. Analytics tools can show which type of content you are posting gets the best results, which platform is working the best for your target audience, and in general, how well you are doing with your marketing efforts.

Specifically, these are the best ways possible that you can use analytics to form your strategy into the best version of itself...

# Key Performance Indicators

A key performance indicator (KPI) is a term used to describe the measure that shows how effective a company is at achieving their business's top objectives. You should be aware of what your social media KPIs are before you take a look at your analytics. When coming to a conclusion on what your KPIs are, think about what your business strategy is in general to get a good indication of what they should be (they should be along the same line).

A good analytics tool will be efficient and effective when it comes to identifying and tracking your KPIs. Ideally, the tool you choose will be easy to understand and use. Social media analytics are useful for showing the true value of your social media marketing efforts and using different types of data as leverage for optimizing your social media strategy.

# Trend-Based Content Targeting

Any trends that show up online and within social media should definitely be used to the advantage of your marketing strategy. Social media analytics can be eye-opening when it comes to finding out which types of products, advertisements, or content in general are getting the most interest from not just your target audience, but from other demographics as well. Your goal should be to create content that gets people interested in and excited about your brand, and knowing what else out there is doing so can surely play to your advantage.

Part of your strategy should be staying on top of the difference between how you want consumers to perceive your brand and how they perceive it in reality. The actual perception of your target audience, in particular, can be found out from the "chatter" floating around on social media. You can keep track of what the word is about your brand by searching for keywords and paying attention to the sentiment behind users' comments and the language they use.

## Platform-Based Content Targeting

One benefit of knowing and keeping track of your KPIs is that they can help you to target key information on the different social media platforms you use for your brand. Having a strong understanding of the performance of your content on each of your profiles is crucial to the success of your marketing strategy.

Like we mentioned earlier, most of the platforms out there now offer their own analytics tools so that you do not have to go out searching for the right one on your own if you do not want to. Facebook Insights and Twitter Analytics are both examples of native analytics tools.

## Personalization

The final area we will discuss when it comes to the usefulness of social media analytics is the personalization of your content and marketing tactics to better match your audience's profiles. Imagine how it would feel to have a brand customize their customer service techniques to meet and anticipate your needs exactly - it would make you feel like you are valued as a customer, would it not?

As already mentioned, creating and posting content by taking a more personal approach and appealing specifically to certain audience members is much more effective than keeping every piece of content generic. Imagine going to a conference and finding that the speakers do not seem to have anything to say that directly applies to you--you would not feel like there was much of a point of attending. But a speaker that hits home with every point that they make would make your attendance well worth the time and money you spent to be there. A personalized experience is always more valuable and beneficial than an impersonal one.

Analytics tools on for social media can help you to create that personalized experience for your entire audience. The data that you find will allow you to find out what content you can and should be creating to be relevant to your followers, ultimately leading to an increase in your ROI.

## Tools Available for Social Media Analytics

Other than the analytics tools that come packed in with your social media profiles, what are the other tools that you could be using that might give even more insight into the function of your marketing efforts? The ones we have listed here are just a few of the best ones available to the public, some of which require payment, but all of which are worth looking into depending on your exact marketing needs.

# Sprout Social

Sprout Social is good for any brand that uses a variety of platforms, as it works with Facebook, Instagram, LinkedIn, Twitter, and Google+. It allows you to manage each of these platforms from one dashboard to make things easier for you, which also means that you can compare information across each platform in one convenient place. Sprout Social offers a 30-day trial for free before requiring a payment of ninety-nine dollars each month.

# Google Analytics

Google Analytics can be used by anyone who uses Google/Chrome as their web browser. Although it is not technically a social media tool, it does offer the ability to track how your social media campaigns are working and measure the ROI of your social media accounts. You can use it to monitor social media use to see the traffic flowing through your different accounts. Because it is built into the Google web browser, it works for any platform that you use for absolutely free. For a similar experience, you could try Adobe Analytics or StarCounter.

# Snaplytics

Because of how simple SnapChat is and the minimal functions it offers, it has the least amount of information to offer when it comes to analytics. The range of functions on SnapChat is fairly small when compared to others like Facebook and Twitter; viewing and commenting on content is pretty much the extent of what SnapChat does (which is not a bad thing, just to be clear).

To gather as much data as is possible from SnapChat, you can use a tool like Snaplytics. This tool will take you as deep as you can go, giving you data on things like your snap performances and the growth rate of your audience. It can also give you information about the performance of your Instagram Stories.

There are not a lot of quality options when it comes to SnapChat analytics tools, but you can also try Delmondo and Storyheap if you would prefer to shop around before committing to one particular tool.

## Iconosquare

If you want to focus on your Instagram marketing strategy performance, try Iconosquare. Starting at nine dollars a month, you can check your photo, video, and story data, and see influencer analytics for a higher price. Similar to Iconosquare, you can try Later (which we have mentioned in an earlier section as a scheduling tool) or Instagram Insights (the analytics tool that is built into Instagram).

## Buzzsumo

Buzzsumo is a little bit different than the other analytics tools in that it examines how your website's content does on social media instead of just how each platform's performance holds up. In other words, it provides a quick and easy way to see how each item on your website does in general instead of having to look at how it does on Facebook, Instagram, Twitter, Pinterest, and LinkedIn (the five platforms it works for). The available plans start at ninety-nine dollars per month - if this seems a little bit too steep for you, you can try Epicbeat or Ahrefs for a similar experience.

## Tailwind

Compatible with Instagram and Pinterest, Tailwind is one of the most popular third-party analytics tools out there. It can be used to track your audience count and engagement (among other features), starting at ten dollars per month. If you use Pinterest for the majority of your social media marketing, you will find Tailwind or a similar tool (like Pinterest Analytics or Viralwoot) to be extremely useful.

## ShortStack

ShortStack is the perfect tool for a brand that does a lot of contests, as it provides information on how each of your contests performed. Using ShortStack can keep you from accidentally wasting time through contests and help you to make the most of each one that you start. It works for Facebook, Twitter, and Instagram, and is one of the most popular contest tools used. You can use ShortStack for free or sign up for a plan (they start at twenty-nine dollars a month), or you can take a look at Gleam or Woobox, which are comparable to ShortStack.

## Squarelovin:

This is a great Instagram app that helps you make the most out of Instagram. It has many useful features but overall, works to help you streamline your Instagram presence and build audience engagement. It helps you find and win over influencers, how to maximize the reach and effectiveness of your content. When used properly, this tool will help you cut the fat on your social media marketing efforts on Instagram. With incredibly insightful reporting, you will be able to see very directly what's working and what isn't and tweak all your campaigns and efforts accordingly.

## *TapInfluence*

The final analytics tool for social media that we will look at is Tapinfluence. This tool is great for any business that uses influencer marketing campaigns, and it works for Facebook, Twitter, Instagram, Pinterest, LinkedIn, and Youtube. You can use Tapinfluence to search for influencers that you might want to work with in the future, or simply to track campaign performance. Alternatively, you could try Traackr or Influency.

No matter which tools you ultimately decide to go with, make sure that they are appropriate for your needs and will benefit your brand the most. There is nothing wrong with trying a few tools out before committing to one. You need to do what is best your brand, and your brand deserves to work at its full potential.

# Chapter 9: Paid Ads vs. Content Marketing

We have already covered a lot of information on producing effective content and achieving good awareness levels on your brand's social media profiles through properly exposing said content. In this section, we will attempt to draw parallels between simple content marketing and paid advertisements in order to help you make an informed decision about whether or not paid ads are the right move for your brand.

The use of social media for marketing purposes is a vital part of your brand's marketing strategy overall. Social media is where people spend a lot of time - they log on to communicate with each other, stay updated on events, and learn new things. Not many people will readily admit it, but some folks actually use social media to find out about new products and services that fit well into their lifestyles. Indeed, social media is becoming more and more of a shopping platform. To not take advantage of this pool of potential customers would be a mistake; regardless of what methods you use to advertise on social media platforms, IT NEEDS TO BE DONE.

Both content marketing and paying for advertisements on social media have been proven to help further the success of brands across the world, so no matter what you pick, you should be able to see a positive effect (assuming proper execution, of course). You will simply need to look at the resources available to your brand and what you cannot do without. For example, what is your total budget for marketing? How many people do you have available to focus on social media, whether that means posting new and recycled content, answering follower inquiries, or sifting through data to better adjust current strategies? Considering the demographics and psychographics of your target audience, how many of your customers follow you on social media compared to other outreach outlets? To be successful in marketing, you need to have a plan.

So, let us take a look at the details of what makes up content marketing and paid social media advertisements.

### How Content Marketing Works

Content marketing can be defined as "a strategic marketing approach focused on creating and distributing valuable, and consistent content to attract and retain a clearly defined audience - and, ultimately, to drive profitable customer action." (reference 25). At the very core of your content marketing strategy should be content that is relevant and informative. Being relevant to your audience is a more effective marketing approach than presenting a direct pitch of whatever it is you can offer customers. Throughout this entire eBook so far, we have gone over the different aspects of quality content; by now, you probably know quality content like the back of your hand.

# Benefits of Content Marketing

In a nutshell, there are three main benefits of content marketing: cost-effectiveness, an increase in sales, and a higher quality of customer. First and foremost, **content marketing is free**. Instead of spending money on advertising, it can be spent on other things, like production or design. Considering the fact that the average small business spends around one-hundred thousand to one-hundred twenty thousand dollars in a single year on advertising (reference 26), free content marketing looks like a pretty good option.

The most important benefit of this method is that **content marketing increases sales**. The content meant to be a part of content marketing is engaging and real, building trust with viewers and helping them to feel like the brand they are looking at really matters. A relationship is built between the viewer and brand that leads to higher sales than advertisements that jump right into what the product or service is and what it is capable of doing for the viewer. A personal relationship is a better motivator than a product-first approach.

A relationship between the brand and its audience also means that **consumer marketing brings in better customers**. As a result of consumer marketing, you can rest assured that your audience is there for you, not just to have their own needs filled. These customers are more likely to be loyal to your brand as your relationship with them grows, which means that in the event of a mistake made on your end, the customer is more likely to offer forgiveness instead of hostility. A higher quality of customer leads to higher revenues for your business.

Bill Gates once said, "Content is where I expect much of the real money will be made on the Internet." Mr. Gates was right on the mark. The content that you produce for your audience is what they come to your page for - you are kidding yourself if you think they are showing up to see more of your advertisements. Valuable content has the ability to drive audience growth higher than you might imagine.

## *Drawbacks of Content Marketing*

Like everything worth doing, **content marketing takes time**. It cannot be something that you only do once and expect to see great results in the future - you need to continually produce interesting content and promote it in such a way that your audience will be intrigued and move in closer. Making sure that your content is interesting enough to hold your audience's attention takes creativity and patience. Content marketing requires commitment; if you want to see progress, you will likely have to schedule in time that you will specifically commit to carrying out the steps in your content marketing strategy.

**Content marketing can feel overwhelming**. It requires a well thought-out plan and committed execution of that plan. You can start with an editorial calendar or schedule so that you can see which pieces you plan to publish each week and/or month - you should have at least one month scheduled in advance to avoid getting backed up. Having a specific deadline for marketing can be stressful if you are not used to having strict boundaries in place. The amount of structure needed for content marketing can make paid advertising seem much more appealing.

Building relationships and trust through **content marketing is a long road**. What we mean by this is that you need to have a sufficient amount of convincing content to win over your audience. So, when you add up the time it takes to make all of this content and publish it without bombarding your audience, as well as the time it takes for your audience to go through each piece and let it affect them, you could be looking at many months, or even years, before a viewer becomes a committed customer. This is a long time to wait and work in order to see progress.

One thing to keep in mind when mulling over the pros and cons of content marketing is that everything comes at a cost, whether that cost is financial or another category. Think about what you are willing to go through and what you are and are not willing to give up for the sake of your brand when you are deciding which approach to take for your marketing strategy.

## Should You Pay for Advertisements on Social Media?

Honestly, if you are satisfied with the amount of traffic you are getting on your brand's social media profiles, you might not see the need of starting to paying for advertisements. Whether or not you use paid ads is completely up to you - there is no rule that says you have to do it to succeed in your industry. However, you could always be doing more to increase your audience reach, and if you have the funds to pay for social media advertising, then it can be well worth it.

The top reasons that people use social media are (1) to keep in touch with friends and family, (2) to stay caught up on world events, (3) to avoid boredom, and (4) to entertain themselves (reference 27). The most effective paid ads will incorporate one or more of these things to more effectively reach their target audience. Why are these the ads that work? Because they are the ones that do not feel like ads at all. They engage the audience before pushing the selling agenda - the needs of the customer come before the needs of the business on the priority list. Failing to put the customer first when creating paid ads on social media (or anywhere, really), can cause the ads themselves to fail.

# What Are Your Options?

One of the first things you will need to decide after committing to paid social media ads is which type of ad you want to try. **Sponsored posts** are posts that are sponsored by a company to boost their viewer count and draw attention to the poster. Essentially, you will pay for this post to get more views by people who are not following you. The platform you are posting on will have tools available for you to use to make sure that your ad is effective.

When you post your ad make sure that you select the audience based on your location and that you are sponsoring a post that contains original content about your brand.

Depending on the platform you use, ads show up in different places, like the sidebar or as part of the newsfeed. **Newsfeed ads** appear naturally and fit in with the content already in the user's newsfeed. Having newsfeed ads increases the likelihood of them being shared by viewers, so they are a great way to increase awareness. **Sidebar ads** are located to the left or right of the newsfeed and remain in the same spot as the individual scrolls through their newsfeed. They do not blend in with regular content, so it is much more obvious to the viewer that their purpose is to sell something. Even so, they can be just as effective as newsfeed ads and will likely cost the same.

One perk of paying for social media ads is that some platforms have partnerships with others that allow them to share ads. These **networking ads** allow people on different networks to see your brand and helps to gather interest on platforms that you did not originally post the ad. These ads tend to be cheaper than the other types because they often get clicked on by mistake (it is sort of like getting a discount).

Remember back when we were talking about reusing content to increase the number of views it gets? You can do the same thing with ads with **remarketing**. This ad method redirects your previous site visitors back to your site later on and can double your revenue. Remarketing basically just acts as a reminder to visit your page the next time they use that particular social media platform, so it is a good way to advertise without being too pushy.

The last paid ad type we will mention here is **influencer marketing**. With influencer marketing, you are paying someone with a large following that you would like to piggy-back off of to mention your brand and nudge their own followers to check out your page. If this is the direction you would like to go in rather than paying the social network itself, you should make sure to go about it in a way that will heighten your chances of success. For example, make sure that you choose an influencer that relates to your brand and who has the same target audience as you do. You will also want to pick an influencer who actively engages with their audience rather than just collects followers. Only pick an influencer who gives you a fair price, and consider making creative deals with them such as performance-based bonuses or share-swapping. This method of paid advertising requires a little bit of background between you and the influencer in order to work - pick someone who knows who you are and has already mentioned you in a comment somewhere before trying to make a deal.

# *SMART Advertising*

The goal of paid advertising is always to extend the reach of your brand and boost your profits, but you need a more specific goal if you really want your ads to work. We make goals all the time, and your marketing strategy for your social media profiles can prosper as the result of proper goal-setting.

Think **SMART** when making your goals: specific, measurable, attainable, relevant, and time-bound. (reference 27). Making a goal as **specific** as possible and making sure it is **measurable** means that it will be much more easily achieved, as it will be more effectively kept track of. Any goal you set should be **attainable**, or within reach, so that you are not setting yourself up for failure from the beginning. Keeping your goals **relevant** means keeping small steps towards your goal relevant to the goal itself. For example, if getting more "likes" on Facebook helps you move closer to the goal of increasing social media revenue, it is relevant. And finally, your goal should be **time-bound**, meaning there should be a clear deadline for your goal to be achieved so that you can more easily be kept on track.

Each of the goals you set to move yourself towards the ultimate goal of increasing brand awareness and revenue should fit together like pieces of a puzzle or threads on a tapestry. With your goals in place, planning your strategy in full can be much more simple. You can use tangible methods of keeping track of your goals, like drawing out a timeline for yourself or setting up a small rewards system to keep yourself motivated. It all depends on what works best for you and your business.

## *Benefits of Paid Ads*

Paid social media is the way to go for maximized visibility for your content. The vast majority of social media marketers report an increase in exposure and traffic through their efforts (reference 28). Simply put, the main benefit of paying for advertisements on social media is that you can reach people that you would not be reaching by your own efforts alone. These ads target people based on what they have already shown interest in and the demographics that they belong to. For example, if your brand focuses on selling clothing to pregnant or nursing women, then the algorithm of whichever platform you are advertising on might target social media users who have searched for other maternity or baby products. Regardless of what your brand is offering, there are other brands out there that relate to you enough for you to piggy-back off of their audience.

# Platform Ad Services

Facebook is *the* social media platform to use if you are trying to build awareness for your brand. The site accounts for one in every six minutes spent online worldwide, after all. Along with sites like Twitter, Instagram, and Pinterest, Facebook can be used to build awareness for your brand and increase your website traffic. As LinkedIn is more of a brand-to-brand (B2B) networking tool, its focus is more on business networking. That being said, it is also used heavily for increase website traffic and brand awareness.

# The Cost of Advertising

Advertising through social media can be relatively inexpensive - Facebook ads, for example, cost an average of less than eight dollars per mille (thousand impressions). There are different payment options depending on the platform being used - you can pay per mille or per click. Of course, each platform reserves their right to set their own price for advertisements, but they remain fair across the platform range. Consulting with a marketing agency can allow you to make the best decisions for your brand in regards to where you should be spending your advertising budget.

# Drawbacks of Paid Ads

Other than the obvious drawback of seeing money leave your company by paying for advertising, there are other drawbacks of paid ads that are specific to each platform (reference 29). While starting up a **Facebook** advertising campaign is easy, affordable, and effective, it can also be time-consuming if you really want it to work to its fullest potential because of the amount of time it takes to monitor their effectiveness. Advertising organically on Facebook seems to be less effective than it once was due to the algorithm changes in their NewsFeed, leading to a higher dependence on paid ads than before.

**Instagram** can also be considered time-intensive and less effective for organic advertising, and their high focus on images and videos rather than text means that the more textually in-depth content cannot be properly promoted on this platform. They also have a much younger demographic of users, with 90% of them being under the age of 35. Their limited audience reach does not allow for a broad range of brands to effectively use Instagram to promote their products and services.

While it is great for different businesses and professionals to interact with one another, **LinkedIn** has its limits in the educational department; the FAQ and Help sections have considerably fewer resources than bigger platforms like Facebook, leaving something to be desired. In order to get where you want to go on LinkedIn, you need to follow a much more lengthy path and risk getting lost or distracted along the way.

**Twitter** is perhaps the most limited platform, as messages are forcibly kept brief with a 140 character limit per tweet. Changes to your feed happen rapidly with so many tweets per minute being posted, which means your ads get pushed farther away at a quicker pace than on other platforms. Ads or promoted posts on Twitter are more often viewed as spam, and many brands fail to fit into Twitter's user base.

As you can see, there are going to be certain drawbacks to whichever platform you choose to use for your social media marketing strategy. It is up to you to weigh the benefits and the drawbacks to deciding where it is worth it to spend your hard-earned money when it comes to advertising. To make things a little bit simpler, you can try putting all of the platforms you are considering into a chart so that you can compare their qualities in an easy-to-view format. Do not be afraid to consult with others as well, as they might have insights that you lack.

## The Winning Combination

In general, advertising on social media can be a tricky business, even with everything provided to you by the platform. Paid ads can be well worth the time, money, and effort put in, but so can organic content marketing. Ideally, your social media marketing strategy would be a combination of content marketing and paid advertisements. Even with their drawbacks, both of these marketing methods have been proven to boost brand awareness across the different social media platforms and increase customer sales. You cannot go wrong by choosing a strategy that incorporates both paid and unpaid methods.

Let's put it another way…

Think about all of the different ingredients that it takes to make a burger. Some of these ingredients, like cheese, onion, and tomato, are delicious on their own and require very little preparation. Other ingredients, like beef and the bun need to have a bit of work done on them to make sure that they are prepared just right. Combining all of these things together makes an exquisite type of food that you would not be able to imagine turning out the same way if one of the ingredients was missing. Bringing together the cooked beef patty, cheese, ketchup, and other ingredients depending on your taste, creating a satisfying end product.

The same principle applies to creating an effective social media marketing strategy - some components on their own are good, but can be made better by combining them with other crucial components. Paid advertising and content marketing on social media go together like peanut butter and jelly; they are a perfect match and work better together than apart. After you know where you want to go with your marketing strategy, you can find which methods of advertising work best for what your brand has to offer and make a name for yourself.

# Conclusion

The average person spends over two hours on social media sites or apps every day. People use social media for communication, education, networking, leisure, and more. It is a great place to stay updated about the things going on in the lives of people around you, as well as current events in your neighborhood, across your country, and even throughout the world. With the amount of time that the majority of people spend online and using social media every day, it only makes sense to use the different platforms available to your brand to market your products and services and grow your business.

During our time together, we have talked about not only the basics of brand building and how to captivate your audience by showcasing your skills and products, but also how to interact with your customers in a way that shows your interest in them both as customers and as individuals. We have learned about the importance of developing a meaningful relationship between your brand and your target audience, and what positive results can follow. We have discussed the different tools available for making your brand's social media accounts stand out among those of your competitors, and the utilities available for the more technical side of marketing. We have covered branding, advertising, networking, and more - everything we could possibly help you with as you aim to get your business off the ground and build up a social media presence from scratch.

Building a brand from the ground up can be a long and arduous process, but what we need to keep in mind is that help is always there if you are looking in the right places. There are countless resources available all over the place, whether you choose to look online or seek the counsel of someone else who has already undergone the processes that are in front of you. Trying to build your business completely out of your own efforts and refusing help can be one of the biggest mistakes you could possibly make.

We want you to succeed in the business world, which is why we cannot stress the importance of an effective social media strategy and positive customer relationships (and even business-to-business relationships) enough. Always remember that your target audience is the lifeblood of your brand; without customers and the needs that they have for your product or service, there would be no point to any of your efforts.

If you follow the guide that we have outlined in this eBook, you will be well on your way to becoming an expert in social media marketing. Remember, any task can be daunting before you have an idea of where to start, but building your understanding of the tasks ahead of you can expel your anxieties and help to propel yourself forward. Do not be afraid to take chances as you build your brand - the rewards that will come out of your efforts will be well worth the risks you took along the way!

# References

1. Statistica, The Statistics Portal. Number of Facebook users by age in the U.S. as of January 2018 (in millions). https://www.statista.com/statistics/398136/us-facebook-user-age-groups/.
2. Start With Why, Simon Sinek. https://startwithwhy.com/.
3. Tools Hero. The Golden Circle, Simon Sinek. https://www.toolshero.com/leadership/golden-circle-simon-sinek/.
4. Mind Tools. SWOT Analysis. https://www.mindtools.com/pages/article/newTMC_05.htm.
5. Social Triggers. List Building 101. How to Build an Email List… …And Actually Make Money From It. https://socialtriggers.com/list-building/.
6. Zapier. What is Drip Marketing? The Complete Guide to Drip Campaigns, Lifecycle Emails, and More. https://zapier.com/learn/email-marketing/drip-marketing-campaign/.
7. Social Triggers. The 7 High-Converting Places to Add Email Sign-Up Forms to Build Your List. https://socialtriggers.com/email-signup-forms-build-list/.
8. Sprout Social. 10 Social Media Branding Strategies Every Business Should Follow. https://sproutsocial.com/insights/social-media-branding/.
9. Photoshop. https://www.photoshop.com/.
10. Canva. https://www.canva.com/.
11. Later. https://later.com/.
12. Sprout Social. https://sproutsocial.com/.
13. Get Bambu. https://getbambu.com/.
14. Sprout Social. 12 Ways to Boost Brand Awareness on Social Media. https://sproutsocial.com/insights/brand-awareness/.
15. Forbes. Which Social Media Platform is the Most Popular in the US? https://www.forbes.com/sites/kevinmurnane/2018/03/03/which-social-media-platform-is-the-most-popular-in-the-us/#5ff080971e4e.
16. Ad Week. Facebook Hits 40 Million Page Milestone, Launches Live Chat for Businesses. https://www.adweek.com/digital/facebook-hits-40-million-page-milestone-launches-live-chat-for-businesses/.
17. The UK Domain. How to grow your social media followers to strengthen your brand. https://www.theukdomain.uk/grow-social-media-followers-strengthen-brand/.
18. Neil Patel. Get More Fans, Followers, and Shares with these 6 Social Media Marketing Tools. https://neilpatel.com/blog/get-fans-followers-shares/.
19. Quick Sprout. How to Convert Your Social Media Followers Into Customers Effectively. https://www.quicksprout.com/2018/04/04/how-

to-convert-your-social-media-following-into-customers-effectively/.

20.    Web Hosting Secrets Revealed. 24 Golden Rules for Social Media Marketers and Bloggers. https://www.webhostingsecretrevealed.net/essential-social-media-marketing-guide/.

21.    KK*. 1,000 True Fans, The Technium. https://kk.org/thetechnium/1000-true-fans/.

22.    Hubspot. 5 Proven Social Media Engagement Strategies for 2018. https://blog.hubspot.com/marketing/proven-social-media-engagement-strategies.

23.    Sprout Social. What Is Social Media Engagement & Why Should I Care? https://sproutsocial.com/insights/what-is-social-media-engagement/.

24.    Sprout Social. 8 of the Best Social Media Analytics Tools of 2018. https://sproutsocial.com/insights/social-media-analytics-tools/.

25.    Content Marketing Institute. What Is Content Marketing? https://contentmarketinginstitute.com/what-is-content-marketing/.

26.    Word Stream, Online Advertising Made Easy. The Comprehensive Guide to Online Advertising Costs. https://www.wordstream.com/blog/ws/2017/07/05/online-advertising-costs.

27.    Lyfe Marketing. Do Paid Social Ads Really Work? You Bet They Do. https://www.lyfemarketing.com/blog/paid-social-ads/.

28.    Blue Corona. Paid Social Media Advertising Campaigns. https://www.bluecorona.com/pay-per-click/social-media-ads.

29.    PPC Hero. Pros and Cons of Top Social Media Advertising Platforms. https://www.ppchero.com/pros-and-cons-of-top-social-media-advertising-platforms/.

www.ingramcontent.com/pod-product-compliance
Lightning Source LLC
Chambersburg PA
CBHW082111220526
45472CB00009B/2138